IN A NEW _____

Be the Self you Truly Are

ANNA HAYWARD

POLAIR PUBLISHING
LONDON

First published September 2011

© Copyright, Anna Hayward 2011

British Library Cataloguing-in-Publication Data
A catalogue record for this book is available from the British Library

ISBN 978-1-905398-25-6

© Copyright, Anna Hayward, 2011

Designed and set by the Publisher in
11.5 on 14 pt Joanna and 9.5 on 14 pt Gill Sans Book
and printed in Great Britain by Cambridge University Press

In a New Light

CONTENTS

Acknowledgments

In the writing this book, I would like to acknowledge the invaluable support
and encouragement of Jeremy Hayward and Jan De Vulder. This book would
also be the poorer if it were not for the skills and particular understanding
of the subject matter of its editor Colum Hayward.

INTRODUCTION

WHY WOULD someone pick up this book to read it? I guess, like most writers, I asked myself this question. As an introduction to what is in these pages, here are some reasons that occurred to me.

You might, of course, just be intrigued by the **TITLE**. Or you might be finding it difficult to understand how people can become CRUEL OR TERRORISTS. Or maybe you have wondered for some time how you can go from being *a loving, sensitive being* to *a screaming banshee* or a cold fish, and back again! Perhaps you are having *difficulties in a relationship*, in which you are being accused of being something you are not, and perhaps you are not sure who you are. Maybe you *want to make things work* in the relationship, but no matter how good your intentions, your difficult feelings still get in the way. You may lack confidence, or suffer from feelings of inadequacy. You may be struggling to find your voice at work—to stand up for yourself—to be yourself, even! You may *long for a relationship*, but feelings of **not being good enough get in the way and make you tongue-tied or awkward**. Or maybe you feel **stuck in a relationship, a job, a place, a feeling, guilt, fear**. Maybe your thoughts go **round and round**, and you feel out of control.

These are just some of the reasons why you may decide to read on.

I hope I have managed in the book to provide a unique approach to how we see ourselves and others. Parts of the psychology are not unique in themselves, and I have referred to a number of writers who offer ways of thinking that I have found work in practice. However, there is a way in which I believe I have integrated a number of approaches, including ones I have developed myself, which present a constructive, holistic way of looking at our selves and at others.

I believe it is a way that offers a totally positive approach to the self, even when things appear to go wrong, or when we think we make mistakes. Through seeing the self in this light, I hope to show how we can live with our imperfections, while moving through them, and how we can understand the 'why' behind the destructive nature, so that we can find ways to help create change.

I have been a practising counsellor for over thirty years, and I have developed an approach to people which I believe is wholly positive, affirmative, reassuring, safe; I am told, too, that it works! I use the same approach when I run workshops for teaching counselling skills and for helping people to see themselves and others in a new light. But I do not believe you *have* to undergo counselling or be part of a group in order to benefit from a book such as this.

Just as this book was due to go to the press, there was a fascinating addition to the literature on this subject, in the shape of Timothy D. Wilson's REDIRECT: THE SURPRISING NEW SCIENCE OF PSYCHOLOGICAL CHANGE. It is too early to assess this book fully, but Wilson's 'story-editing' approach to 'redirecting' people's ideas of themselves and their lives seems to be another strand of understanding consistent with this book's assertions. For example, he insists that it is possible to so change our views of ourselves that we can gradually but significantly change how we act and what we achieve, but through a simple process, and not through endless and expensive therapy.

I have offered some exercises throughout the book (as well as three longer ones in the Appendix) and called them 'New Light'. You may find these helpful, but this is not intended to be a book you have to work through in order to use it effectively. It is in putting the ideas into practice in your everyday life that you will discover whether this works for you. The point is that even just reading a psychology which is positive, accessible and unthreatening can transform how you feel about yourself, and how you relate to others. However, this way of thinking is different from so much of the conventional wisdom held in our various social groupings today, both culturally and psychologically, so that—if you find it helpful—you may need to keep reminding yourself of the main premises.

In the traditional analogy, you cannot tell what the whole elephant is like just by seeing its tail—and so too with the ideas presented in this book. Each section is part of a whole that is better perceived when all have been read!

I am under no illusions that changing the way you view yourself and others, even when you agree with the philosophy, is something which often happens overnight. However, one of the main ideas offered in this book is that when things seem not to work or seem to go wrong, with a different handle on them you are able to see that you have always been more than perhaps you have ever thought.

Seeing yourself in this new light can help you to live positively with yourself, as you are now, and in so doing find your own way forward from there. Ultimately this book is about faith in you.

Anna Hayward
Summer 2011

CHAPTER ONE

WHAT IS YOUR VIEW
OF YOURSELF?

*Our deepest fear is not that we are inadequate. Our deepest fear is
that we are powerful beyond measure.*

MARIANNE WILLIAMSON

SINCE you picked up a book about seeing yourself in
a new light, it might be that you are dissatisfied with
how you see yourself at the moment. Of course,
your response may vary according to what is happening
in your life at this moment. I hope, though, that as you
read on you might find another viewpoint that will bring
you greater confidence, self-respect and freedom. In fact
it has been my experience that people do not feel very
good about themselves, particularly at difficult times—
and yet, hiding behind that judgment, there is a part of
the self that knows they are more than they appear to be.

In counselling work I sometimes find it helpful, at the
appropriate time for the individual, to ask them to tell
me what they like about themselves, or what they think is
good about themselves. People not only find it hard to do
this, but find it hard even to think about doing so without
embarrassment and even pain. Some of that reaction may
be to do with the difficulty we have saying positive things

about ourselves in the presence of others: the myth that it is somehow arrogant to do so.

That very reaction tells us quite a lot about the psychology that surrounds us. By this I mean the popular concept the Western world has about how we think and are motivated, and the influences that can have on our feelings and relationships as we mature. In fact, there are other ways of looking at who we are and how things happen in life, ways which I hope to reveal through this book.

Let's return to your view of yourself. I've listened to many people telling me about their self-view, and the list of words that follows summarizes some of the things you may share. When you are at a low ebb you might be more immersed in the negative ones, but I suspect that many people feel a variety of these things all the time, beneath their outward persona, and that often the outward persona is an attempt to protect the sensitive inner self from harm. So can I suggest that inside you might feel

- *vulnerable*   **anxious or worried**
  - sensitive   *>insecure<*   <u>a failure</u>
- unsure,   **uncomfortable**,   *limited*,
  - [isolated]   lacking in confidence
    - {misunderstood}   **guilty**,
  - *self-critical*   <u>helpless</u> and **overwhelmed**?

You may not feel all of these at once, and you may not recognize that they are there until a crisis happens, or you lose someone or something you cherish, but they find a way to bubble up nonetheless!

It may also be that underneath you feel **angry**, <u>resentful</u>, **bitter** or *cynical*. As you will read later, these feelings can come about as a direct result of the first list. To tell you not to experience guilt about having these feelings may make you want to throw the book at the wall! Guilt, it seems, is a feeling which frequently underpins our lives, and particularly when one has or has had any religious faith. I hope to show how unrealistic guilt is as a deterrent, and how counterproductive it is to wellbeing.

There is a salutary cartoon by the US cartoonist Tom Wilson, creator of the comic strip 'Ziggy', in which the figure of Freud is sitting with pad and pencil looking at his client lying on a couch. The client is giving this answer to a question: 'I'd try to be my own best friend ... but I fear rejection!'

However...

...there are also times when you know how UNIQUELY WONDERFUL you are—though you may not outwardly recognize or admit it. Often those times coincide with and are the result of **being in love**, feeling appreciated or praised, PRODUCING SOMETHING YOU FEEL PROUD OF, *doing something which requires* courage, compassion or kindness, *overcoming something difficult or a fear*, learning something new or a new skill, being impressed by something you witness, or being uplifted by something beautiful. At such moments you are reminded of who you really are, without perhaps realizing it; reminded how much you are capable of and of the beauty of the human spirit.

That this sense of ourselves is in the main disregarded or rarely unrecognized seems to me a great sadness, and the cause of much that goes wrong in our lives. Part of what this book hopes to do, therefore, is to reconnect the reader with the knowledge of their own unique greatness. Again, I can imagine a resistance to that word 'greatness', but I'd ask you to try not to resist it! There are some words you may recognize that are often (actually wrongly) attributed to Nelson Mandela:

Our deepest fear is not that we are inadequate. Our deepest fear is that we are powerful beyond measure. It is our light, not our darkness, that frightens us most. We ask ourselves, 'Who am I to be brilliant, gorgeous, talented, and famous?'. Actually, who are you not to be? You are a child of God. Your playing small does not serve the world. There is nothing enlightened about shrinking so that people won't feel insecure around you. We were born to make manifest the glory of God that is within us. It's not just in some of us; it's in all of us. And when we let our own light shine, we unconsciously give other people permission to do the same. As we are liberated from our own fear, our presence automatically liberates others.*

Hearing this, what most of us want to know is why, given that we are 'powerful beyond measure', there is still this sense of inadequacy and helplessness within us? Understanding why may help us to know how to release it, so that the true greatness, creativity and strength can emerge unveiled.

*From Marianne Williamson, A RETURN TO LOVE: REFLECTIONS ON THE PRINCIPLES OF A COURSE IN MIRACLES, but often quoted as though from Nelson Mandela's 1994 Inaugural speech.

CHAPTER TWO

THE LEARNING EDGE

All creation, as any artist will tell us, is a risk. When we learn we take risks—we stretch ourselves and our abilities to the limit; we make a mess, try different routes, different methods. Sometimes we get in a muddle and have to go back to basics. Sometimes we make big errors of judgment, but are they really errors if they show us precisely what not to do, and allow us to see what we really want to achieve?

IN THIS chapter and the next, 'Unveiling the Self to the Self', I want to explore some changes in viewpoint which present an image of the self that is different from much received psychology. All these sections are intended to demonstrate how the statement that we are 'powerful beyond measure' can be believed, despite what seem to be opposite feelings, experiences, stories and contentions, which abound in us and in our world.

What Mistakes Really Are

I SHOULD like to begin by looking at what mistakes really are, since the sense that we have failed often results in a lack of trust in our strength, or in our ability to be loving.

Inside ourselves, it develops oversensitivity, while outside it produces defensiveness.

One of the simplest ways to discuss failure is through something which nearly all of us are familiar with. That is our education. The image of life as a schoolroom is one which is familiar to many. I want to take this thought further, and consider the nature of learning, for another area of my work has been as a teacher of children and adults. In this role I have had to spend a good deal of time contemplating and being aware of how people learn best, and what is happening when learning is taking place.

Consider learning a new skill—let us say, playing the violin. In the process, some most unpleasant noises are produced! You may feel clumsy; half the time you have no idea what you are supposed to be doing. The mind and the fingers can seem to have become disconnected, so that you make mistakes constantly. Yet when you have some experience, there is no point in going on playing the simple pieces you know, and so you drive yourself, or are challenged by your teacher, continuously to play at the limit of your ability, in order to push the boundaries further. This means that you *still* make mistakes—you are constantly making mistakes, because there seems no end to the learning. The noises produced can still sound frightful!

Take this analogy and compare it to the schoolroom of our lives. In order to learn, and to go on learning, we are often on the edge of what might appear to be chaos. Learning is like carving a path through a jungle. You can choose to stay in the clearing, if you like, but you don't learn anything new, and you don't get anywhere. Or you can walk out into the jungle, where you are constantly falling down, tripping up, losing your way, feeling unsure, clumsy, stupid, and constantly making mistakes and having to retrace your steps. But through these mistakes learning comes to you. Growth comes, and new vistas open out.

This is the nature of our schoolroom. Why blame ourselves, then, when we make mistakes? Mistakes are the necessary tools of creation—of finding new life. All creation and discovery begins at the moment of pain and chaos.

And all creation, as any artist will tell us, is a risk. When we learn, we take risks—we stretch ourselves and our abilities to the limit, we make a mess, we try different routes and different methods. Sometimes we get in a muddle and have to go back to basics. Sometimes we make big errors of judgment, but are they really errors if they show us precisely what not to do, and allow us to see what we really want to achieve?

There can be no learning without chaos, risk and mistakes. When most of us are in that learning state we can feel hopeless, confused, a failure, guilty, useless and impatient. However, we do not learn so well if we get lost in those feelings. They make learning much harder, because they sap our confidence and our will to continue. If you felt those feelings constantly when learning the violin you would soon give up!

But we cannot give up on life's learning. It doesn't let us. So instead of feeling blame, guilt, impatience, despair and confusion, now's the time to remember from what I have just said that we are **'creative works in progress'**. We have to live on the edge of chaos in order to be on the edge of creation. We make mistakes because they are part of the constant scenery of this place on the edge. Happily, it is precisely through this process and these mistakes that we eventually triumph. The strongest aspects of our nature are developed by the hardest lessons we have had to learn. Through them, our whole consciousness expands.

To regard what we traditionally think of as mistakes as a fundamental part of learning does not, I believe, make us lazy. Rather, it releases us from the prison of guilt and shame, so that we can learn. A person who suffers from chronic self-doubt and self-blame is stuck with the original 'mistake', and the way forward is clouded for them. In order to grow as human beings, to expand our consciousness, our circle of friends, or abilities and our self-expression, we need to embrace the notion that so-called 'failure' is part of that process.

A simple story that illustrates this idea is the familiar one of a break-up of a relationship—usually initiated by just one of the partners—and the pain which ensues for the other. Let's call the one who precipitates the break-up Jo, and her partner Josh. At the time, Jo may well feel guilty for causing Josh pain. Josh may well feel that he has failed. Both go through a difficult time dealing with these feelings. A few years later, Jo is having the time of her life working in another country and Josh is happily married to Jill. Could these new levels of experience have happened without the break-up? Where is the failure, on either part? Hopefully both will have learned more about relationships, too. For example, Jo may have learned to be true to herself and Josh may have learned to let go.

However, if Jo gets stuck with her guilt and Josh with his self-doubt, then it will not only make the parting more problematic and complex, but inhibit their ability to move on. This is where a change of perspective from the conventional norms—a change of psychological awareness about what is happening—will benefit all concerned.

I can offer another example from my teaching experience. I was once engaged as a supply teacher while another was absent through illness. It was Monday morning, and I had a class of eight-year-olds. Before we could start the day, I was reminded by a child that they had a spelling test every Monday morning. When doing supply teaching it is helpful not to interrupt the class teacher's systems too much, so I gave them the test.

I was about to collect their papers at the end when the same child reminded me that their teacher always read out the answers for them afterwards. When this was finished, the child also said that their teacher always asked the class for their scores. I have some issues about scores and tests and my heart sank, knowing that some children would be at the 'bottom', and that by making that public they would be shamed, or forced into a defensive pose.

We began with the top scores—ten out of ten, and on down. When we got to about six out of ten I had an inspiration. I began to praise the children more: 'Wonderful. That's really good'. Looking around at puzzled faces I added: 'You've now got four ways to improve and learn'. This went on until the lowest scorer had nine ways to grow and the praise was even more effusive! I really believe that we can be that pro-active about the creative opportunity our so-called failures offer us.

One rarely knows whether these things work, but walking along the corridor after the class I was behind two of the boys. I heard one say to the other, with great enthusiasm and joy: 'It's great. I've got eight ways to get better!'

New Light: SPOTTING PATTERNS

Can you look back at the mistakes you think you have made in your life with a different perspective, like I have shown? In doing this you might come across a pattern—perhaps a mistake you keep on making, or a circumstance in which you always tend to act the same way, even though you regret it afterwards. I hope that as you continue to read you will begin to see how these patterns come about and explore what triggers the same reaction in you every time, so that you can deal with it. Looking deeper than the surface is part of what this book seeks to offer—a way out of guilt or feelings of hopelessness.

Learning and Change

LEARNING does not stop, of course, with the end of schooling or college, but is something we continue to do all our lives, sometimes without being aware of it. Learning is a basic survival mechanism, as well as a means of growth. For one thing, as we get older we have to learn to cope with changes on all levels: changes in ourselves, our surroundings, our social and familial network and in society. The ability to embrace change is vital to mental and emotional health. In the example of Jo and Josh, a break-up in an intimate relationship was still a major change for both partners to go through, even though it released them. There are many other changes which are less dramatic, maybe more insidious, but we are nonetheless aware of them, inside—particularly when we are feeling openly vulnerable.

Over the years I have counselled many people who are dealing with a change they did not foresee, changes which they are afraid of, changes which are unpleasant, or—the other side of the coin—the feeling of being stuck. To embrace the change in a positive way, and to feel in control as well as free, is a task many set themselves when they are going through a counselling process. In order to feel secure the person needs to find some anchor, some way of staying centred and true to themselves while they are moved by the winds and waves of change.

While I was writing this book, BBC television showed a programme called 'The Secret Life of Waves'. During it the presenter, David Malone, interviewed a number of scientists and surfers about the nature of waves. I was struck, as he was, by a comparison between waves and human beings. Both are the result of energy passing through them. This energy is what causes the water to take on the shape of the wave and to move, and what causes the human being to live and to change. Yet something that is placed on the surface of a wave (in an experiment at Cambridge University they had little yellow and blue ducks!) only moves forwards relatively slowly in comparison to the wave of energy moving beneath it, and is only thrown dramatically forward when the wave expends its energy on the beach.

Surfers talk in the same terms about learning to ride the wave as it changes beneath them, so as not to be thrown by it. The thing about surfers is that they are not lifeless flotsam, but have will and energy themselves to sense the changes and use them to advantage. Watching surfers move makes me understand how much they must have faith in their ability, otherwise it would not work. In counselling, the person has often discovered that the stabilizer for them as they ride the waves of change is an unexpected belief in their own integrity. **It's the arising of their own sense of self.**

Integrity and Our Uniqueness

THE WORD 'integrity' comes from a root that means 'a thing complete in itself'. It is this self-relatedness which distinguishes one of us from another—our uniqueness. In your relation to the self, you are whole, without the need for external direction or comparison. It is my belief that integrity is the natural state for each one of us and that correction, balance and control do not need to be imposed, but are 'built in'—they are part of what it is to be human. The sense the surfer has of how he or she stands relative to the wave is just the same: it cannot be implanted but is an ability that arises from precisely what he or she senses underfoot.

A person, like a plant, will always move towards the light if it is obvious to them. When obstacles impede the progress for a while, both will make detours and come back to the original direction of growth. After pruning, they will grow according to their inherent pattern in as balanced a way as possible. I would maintain that when a person is behaving in a way which appears destructive, either to themselves or others, then somehow either the light is obscured, or the destructive path appears to be a move in the direction of maintaining as much self-worth as possible—perhaps it will be the only course of action that seems possible to the body self.

The body self, and by this I mean the whole collection of body, feelings and mind,* has the task of keeping us safe. To this end the body self can be very protective. Sometimes it does this necessarily and in a way that is visibly useful, but sometimes it does it in ways that are harmful at another level to the self, or damaging to those things and people it perceives as threats.

Essential integrity means that each one of us is unique and there can be no comparison of one person with another. However, many of the institutions, social activities and educational systems in our society depend on making comparisons. Usually they create some kind of hierarchy of worth that each of us knows, deep inside, is spurious. It is no wonder, though, that people make the comparisons and then judge themselves on all levels, and so often find themselves wanting. Another phrase for this would be that they cannot access their integrity.

If everyone could truly believe in their integrity, the fear each has of not being good enough in relation to others would dissolve. There would be no need to for any of us to fight for what we believe. There would be no need to be defensive, because that certainty about the essence of the self would itself bring confidence and knowledge of self-worth. Creatively, that knowledge of our inherent

*I shall continue to refer to the body-self throughout, always meaning body, mind and feeling, and later (p. 54) shall distinguish it from 'the person' or 'the person self'.

and incomparable worth makes us want to live up to it. Moreover, through understanding the truth of our own integrity we would also know it is true for others.

People compare themselves unfavourably with others because they see only the outside of a person, not what is going on underneath. Recently, I was watching the British television soap, 'Casualty'. A boy at school was being forced to take part in cross-country running. He believed he was the only one who couldn't run and the only one who didn't enjoy it; he thought he was different from all the rest. He saw the other boys running past him looking self-assured and happy, and so he assumed that they were

---

New Light UNIQUENESS

Take a few moments to contemplate your uniqueness as something to be celebrated. Imagine all comparisons set aside, all cultural norms released, and all the ways in which you may be tempted to think of yourself as not good enough when compared with others gone.

Someone not born on this planet would look at the variety of human beings, including you, and not see someone wanting in any way. They would someone different, of course—but they would have no means of comparison, no norms, and therefore they would be free to see you as you are.

If there is any situation in your life where comparison with others is an issue for you, take yourself into that situation in your mind and imagine how it would feel to stand proudly as a unique person—your own dear self, without fear. You are the centre of your own universe—you have your own voice, your own body, your own mind, your own feelings—you are, quite simply, unique.

feeling fine about the running and doing well, because of how they appeared.

One day, the boy runs past the reflective glass of a bus shelter, and as he does so he looks across at himself. At that moment he realizes that he comes across just like all the other boys. The actor and camera managed to convey in that one glance the impression that maybe many of the other boys felt just like he did inside, but they did not show it outwardly any more than he did. Much insecurity comes from the tendency to measure ourselves against our perceptions of others, not against how they really are. As this story shows, the truth can be completely different.

The constant exchange of energy with our environment and with others can give us the feeling that we are only flotsam, or just a small bit of a wave that is pulled along by others and by circumstance. Understanding ourselves as unique, and realizing that our integrity is not dependent on what is around us or what happens to us means that we begin to reconnect with an internal sense of self which is not reliant on things staying the same. It is not reliant on how much we know now, because even through our mistakes we can learn, and certainly it is not reliant on what others think of us.*

People are Not what they Seem

IN THE NEXT three sections I would like to present an idea I have likened to the symbol of the yin/yang. This shows two teardrop shapes

*For a process designed to reclaim your sense of being in control see the exercise in Appendix I, 'Riding the Waves of Change'.

fitted cleverly into one another inside a circle, as in the picture. Hidden within the white teardrop is a little circle of black and conversely inside the black teardrop is a little circle of white. Now, just imagine that this symbol is in three dimensions so that the teardrops surround their inner globes of white and black completely. Now you won't be able to see them. This is how people can appear—the outside being quite different from what the individual may actually be feeling or thinking inside.

It's hard to believe this when you are facing any kind of situation where the person in front of you is defensive— for example, if you are dealing with a relationship problem, being criticized, feeling hurt by someone or feeling guilty. At the moment when your child is screaming at you because it wants something you do not want to give it, can you look at the child and think, '***This is a wonderful being—how amazing he is***'? At the moment when your boss is coldly criticizing you for something which is not your fault, can you look at her and think, 'She is finding this as difficult as I am'? At the moment when parent or partner is blaming you for something you have done to upset them, can you think to yourself, '***How can I help this person feel safe with me***'? At the moment when you are feeling guilty for having done something you regret, can you look at yourself and say, 'I am always doing my best'? Each of these situations asks something of us it feels almost impossible to give.

What appears on the outside of the person at those difficult moments does not seem to be wonderful. What is on the outside is someone who appears the opposite of wonderful—someone who is perhaps angry, needy or defensive. I'd like to suggest that the adage, **'appearances can be deceptive'**, is very true, and that when the person is behaving in such ways, they are in fact entirely different inside. They may be feeling hurt, or afraid. They may be feeling vulnerable or they may have developed a pattern of defensiveness that they feel is appropriate in order to maintain their authority—which possibly means that a threat to their authority is something they fear, of course! They may not even recognize their vulnerability, although they will certainly feel uncomfortable.

You probably have a picture in your mind already of one of the scenes I have described, one where you are before an angry and defensive human being. Imagine what would happen to your feelings if, in the middle of their anger, the person in front of you began quietly and genuinely to cry? On most occasions if that happened your heart would be stirred; your compassion for them would arise. You would in fact get a glimpse of what was really going on underneath all the anger, or coldness. Suddenly, you would know why they were being defensive; you would see their vulnerability, you would remember what it feels like to be hurt yourself, and without hesitation you would try and comfort them. From a position of responding defensively to their anger, at the moment they cried you would probably quite quickly move to saying how sorry you were, even if the situation was not your fault.

I hope what I have said exemplifies what is really going on all the time for people. We are very rarely what we seem on the outside. People are much more vulnerable and afraid than is obvious, because when they are vulnerable, most people put up their greatest or most complex defences. If you live in a flat country by the sea, you build higher dykes than if you live on a hill. You protect yourself against the threat as you perceive it, and the more vulnerable you feel, the higher and stronger those barriers will be! Most of the time in your flat country you will not be thinking about the barriers at all—they will just be there ready to re-pel the sea. But when the storms rage you will pile an extra sandbag here, and another one there, and anyone looking from the outside will see a veritable barricade, maybe not realizing that behind lies a beautiful garden which you are trying to keep safe. I believe that this applies to everyone.

New Light WE'RE ALL VULNERABLE

Think of the person who most scares you, and then the one who makes you most critical or angry, and think next of the person who seems to you to be outwardly most in control and strong. Even that person is vulnerable, in ways you may never witness, but which are as real as your own vulnerability. That person needs as tender handling as the person who is obviously insecure, may-be more. Imagine what hurts might lie beneath an exterior that seems cold and threatening—what vulnerability has caused such a strong defence to be in place! Imagine that person crying.

Remember that the point of doing this is not to make them seem small in your eyes, but so that you may begin to feel a change in power within you—so that you begin to feel more equal with them, less afraid, less vulnerable, more in control.

No matter what is visible on the outside, people are al-most always more vulnerable than you think. You can look at an arrogant person and think they are as tough as can be, yet if you scratch the surface you will find out why they appear that way, and that their arrogance is often based on insecurity and fear. These may be deeply buried, but if they have to deal with tragedy, for example, their insecurity is often revealed. When I have been with clients, many have shared their despair about themselves for feeling critical, being angry or acting unkindly. On those occasions I have asked questions, where appropriate, such as: 'What hurt or fear lies underneath that criticism, that anger, that un-kindness?'. In every case, with time and as long as they have felt neither threatened nor criticized by me,* they have discovered a vulnerability which the anger, criticism or unkindness is seeking to protect. I will discuss how and why I think this happens in the next section.

In total contrast, people are also much stronger, kinder and more creative than they sometimes appear. This mani-fests in crisis situations, either when there is a need to be strong, or when figuratively or actually they are called upon to rescue someone else. I expect that many people have anecdotes of the occasions when either they them-selves or others who were present have acted in incred-ibly surprising ways for good, or been extraordinarily courageous, persevering or patient in the gravest of cir-cumstances, or have found reservoirs of strength or love where beforehand none were thought to exist—whether in a small or a large context.

Protectiveness and Safety

NEXT, I should like to explore what is actually happening when we think critically, act unfeelingly, or speak unkind-

*See the section 'One to One' in chapter eight for ways in which this is done.

ly. In order to protect ourselves from hurt, and out of fear and difficult experiences, we develop around ourselves the defensive walls I've described. We do it in different ways, and from a young age. Collectively these walls are virtually the same as the outward personality people in their daily encounters with us initially contact. The visible personality is composed of whatever we need around us to feel protected and safe, not simply physically, but emotionally and mentally as well.

For example, when we experience someone being defensive, verbally perhaps, we are seeing an obvious example of what is there all the time in varying degrees—a barrier against possible hurt, arising out of fear. You could liken it, as I have said, to a dyke protecting the vulnerable land behind. From outside one only sees the high wall, not the beautiful land which lies beyond, which the person is seeking to protect. As Kennedy and Charles have said in their book ON BECOMING A COUNSELLOR*, 'The things about people that drive us crazy are the things that are keeping them sane'.

My first counselling/clienting training was with Re-evaluation Co-Counselling (the original technique, devized by Harvey Jackins, which I shall refer to henceforth as RC). We were trained in the art of seeing at least two things at once in each person—the outward, defensive behaviour, based on fear and lack of self-respect (called 'the pattern'), and the fundamental 'person'. Both, we were taught, were worthy of respect in their own ways: the outer self for its skilfulness in seeking to protect the vulnerable inner self, and the inner self for its essen-

*See Appendix III, 'Books Mentioned or Recommended'.

tial, unique beauty and intelligence.

Many times I would watch unlovely outward behaviours melt in the light of the 'unconditional positive regard'* of the counsellor. Of course, there were other techniques employed—non-judgmental, attentive listening and help in releasing painful emotions, for example—but whatever happened, the counsellor would keep uppermost in their consciousness the awareness that any defensive behaviour can be listened to with respect and love, because of faith in the underlying goodness and strength of the person. To my mind this is a masterly approach to counselling, and can be applied to all our relationships with others, not only to therapeutic situations.

I believe that one of the fundamental misconceptions of our age is that it takes punishment and the tension of guilt somehow to spur us on to being better. On the contrary, not just in my counselling role but as a teacher I would see a process at work, in which the power of respect and love for even the naughtiest child transformed their behaviour. **Being believed in created safety.** There was no longer the need to protect and to rebel. The defensive crust dissolved and the real person of the child—the innocence if you like—became once more apparent. This, to me, is love in action. Any kind of criticism, any kind of shame stimulates the defensive self in some way—and will only add to the potentially obstructive 'wall' around the true self. Love in action is not colluding with it. There are many skilful ways of saying: 'I do not like your behaviour; I do not think it acceptable, but I respect you'.

Let's take another example, from the world of athletics.

*One of the tenets of RC.

Obviously the various events are about who can win, but they are also very much about how athletes cope with losing. What happens to an athlete psychologically when they fail, let's say in the high jump, at a particular height they may have jumped many times before? What is it that they then need to have and to do to carry on and be successful again? They absolutely need to believe in themselves. They need to believe in their ability. They need to learn from the mistakes they made at the last jump—maybe move their take-off marker a little closer to the bar—and then let all thoughts of that last jump go. They need to stay steady and focused on what they wish to achieve, and not be deterred or influenced by the memory and all that is going on around them. They need to jump their own jump and that jump alone. The runner needs to run his or her own race. In the end, the athletes are not competing against each other, but against themselves. And if they come eighteenth instead of first, training demands that they be philosophical about it and persevere with their practice, and so stay in good shape for the next competition.

We are all like athletes, in that it takes a certain amount of experience and a new light to realize that emotion, chastisement, fear, comparison, lack of self-belief and impatience do not produce the results in the end.

Wrong?

WHEN you view what happens within yourself, and recognize that life is about learning, not failing, and that negativity is protectiveness, not wickedness, you realize that you don't actually get things 'wrong'. However, for some there can be an imbalance so profound as to produce dangerous, antisocial outcomes. I should like to address that briefly, too.

As I've already intimated, I think that there is still a tendency in the media and education, despite many advances, and in the psychology of our culture—both sides of the Atlantic—to think of people in punitive, positive-and-negative terms. By this I mean that there is still, somewhere, a notion that human beings are fundamentally sinful unless corrected. That's the kind of philosophy exemplified in William Golding's story, 'The Lord of the Flies'. It's the notion that if we take away the 'sticks' and the incentives, the punishments and the strictness, we will end up savaging each other and descending into a pit of self-destructiveness—the lesser evils of which might be selfishness, egotism, greed, lust, apathy and sloth. Whenever we are shown awful deeds of cruelty, persecution and injustice this view is naturally deepened.

Using the RC model, however—referred to by Harvey Jackins as the 'pattern and the person', we might begin to see that those who are on a self-destructive path that inevitably affects others could well be acting on their patterns and their defensiveness, and that that in turn arises out of deep fears, pain and insecurity.

To think thus is not to condone any act that causes pain, but it does afford us a way to reform, rather than admit despair, and on many levels: societal, educational, and psychological as well as individual.

To look at all society from this viewpoint would be the subject of a different, much larger book. What is important right here is that society is made up of individuals, and when we remember that, one of the important things we realize is that we all have the ability to be defensive, as well as the ability to unveil our greatness. To understand this within ourselves aids our ability creatively to bring about those conditions which mitigate the defensiveness and bring out the greatness.

When as individuals we begin to find out what our own defensiveness arises from, and as we begin to understand our own sensitivity and release our pain and fears—as we start to show our greatness, you might even say—so each one of us can become more and more creatively constructive in our approach to relationships and to society.

CHAPTER THREE

UNVEILING THE SELF
TO THE SELF

*This is the strength you will one day acknowledge as yours. This is
how you will be one day on all levels of life, but remember you are
great now, and you are lovable in all your imperfection.*

A PHRASE I like to use to describe the process of
self-discovery is 'Unveiling the Self to the Self',
and it seems the right heading for this whole
chapter. Partly I wish to expand on the idea that we are
not as we may seem. However, the crucial point of the
title is to present the notion that this new light in which
you can see yourself is not something extraneous to you,
not something which some people have and others do
not, not something which you have to develop, create or
acquire—but rather something innate, which has been
there all the time and from the beginning of your life, but
which is often covered up—*veiled*.

This notion in itself may come as a new perception,
and I hope that it allows you to see yourself not as wanting, but as whole. The process of unveiling, which I hope
this book will initiate for you, reveals more and more of
the innate strength and beauty of your unique self. I have

chosen to look particularly at intelligence and goodness, since these are areas where people have most often said to me that they feel inadequate.

Conscious and Unconscious

MANY forms of counselling and psychotherapy talk in terms of a conscious and an unconscious self. This section is intended to give a different perspective, one from which nothing is regarded as really unconscious, but things are veiled. To explain a bit more what the veils are, I mean that other things, including our own defensiveness, can get in the way and occlude (shade or hide) our memories, our understanding and even our feelings, but when we feel safe enough we are able to look at ourselves as we are and remember or see behind the veil.

My view is that any seeming lack of truth, confusion, contradiction or uncertainty comes about because of this veil. The veil is composed of negative thoughts and feelings about the self of the kinds mentioned earlier—quite possibly inculcated by contact with others. Lack of trust in the self, for example, will mean you will doubt your decisions and even your ability to make decisions. You can see how uncertainty and confusion arise within.

The veil is also composed of feelings of lack of safety. These cause the defences of the self to be more to the fore, and thus interrupt and obscure the thought processes. In this case, one is living life on the defence—sometimes this means on the offensive—and much that happens is seen in terms of one's patterns. We see ourselves as the hurts and fears, rather than clearly, as the person we really are. We may know how we are being, but we do not perhaps know why, and that is another sort of veil—one which this book seeks to remove.

As a final comment, **I use the word 'veil' because a veil is not an impenetrable barrier and neither is it opaque.** A veil is always, to a certain extent, transparent. In other words, we know ourselves even through the veil. It is that inner knowing which drives us to read books like this, and which makes us feel misunderstood when people only see our defences.

Intelligence is Inherent

ONE OF the ways in which people see themselves unfavourably is around their intelligence. Sadly there are many people who feel lacking in confidence because of what they were told as children: 'You'll never amount to anything!', 'Can't you do better than that?', 'Your brother passes his exams, why can't you?', 'Can't you get anything right?'. Of course, adults make these remarks in frustration from time to time, but I am thinking of people I have counselled where the remarks have gone on for a significant period of time, and have then been augmented by teachers.

A child may grow up gradually feeling more and more inferior, even stupid, with those kinds of remarks ringing in the back of their minds. In the process, all their natural intelligence is curbed. As the child becomes an adult, that natural intelligence (the ability to think and perceive, to explore and create) makes itself felt, yet the adult cannot trust himself or herself enough to let it out or use it. Possibly he does not put himself forward for the best jobs. She does not challenge herself in any way, but stays with things she knows. Perhaps he always goes with what the 'gang' think, even when he secretly has other views. What she may not realize is that she finds all kinds of clever ways of avoiding her big fear, of hiding what she thinks are her weaknesses and of maintaining a feeling of belonging. He is using his intelligence, but without realizing it for what it is.

An education system that encourages a hierarchy of success means that there are only going to be a few people at the top of the scale, and many people in the middle and even more at the bottom. Unfortunately, because 'being top' is so revered, being in the middle or even in second place is not 'good enough', with the result that even people who are considered intelligent do not think of themselves that way at all.

I am not, to be clear, equating education with intelligence—not by any means—but in my experience many people do. The subject of what intelligence is may be a topic for a pure philosophy book, but for the purposes of 'seeing yourself in a new light' it is worth stating how I perceive it. How about: **'Intelligence is the ability to respond creatively and appropriately in the moment'**? That might mean the ability to find out what you need to know, if you don't know it straight away. It might mean the ability to explore a variety of options. It might mean the ability to open the mind. It might mean the ability to see what is in front of you, free from expectations, history and cultural norms. It might mean the ability to try and keep on practising. It might just mean the ability freely and without prejudice, to sense (that is, see, hear, touch, taste, feel) and to think about what you sense, without limitation.

What I am trying to underline here is the idea that intelligence is universal and innate. The word 'inherent', which I used in the chapter title, means that is an essential constituent or characteristic of every one of us. It is not something vouchsafed to a few, but something we all have.

Whether you believe that or not, I have watched people's intelligence blossom along with their self-confidence. I have watched people who begin to believe in themselves achieve what they never believed they could.

New Light UNIQUE INTELLIGENCE

You have the ability to respond creatively in every moment of your life—it is inbuilt. You only have to recognize it. Think of all the myriad moments which make up your daily life, where you make choices, think, respond, feel, avoid, protect, flow out, hold back—all the innumerable actions which constitute living. Focus on an area where you feel stuck, inhibited, unintelligent, unsure. In order to unveil your natural ability, think first of your uniqueness. No one will respond in quite the same way as you, no one will have quite the same perception—you have something therefore to offer which is distinctive. Think of your own individual response to the situation, irrespective of what anyone else may be thinking or doing. Therein lies your intelligence.

Unveiling

WHAT is it that responds to 'unconditional positive regard'; what is it that is revealed in the most challenging situations, but the true, inner strength of the self—that 'greatness' of which my quotation on p. 16 speaks? I'm sure one reason that it has become attributed to Nelson Mandela is that he so well embodies that true, inner strength.

When you feel uplifted or encouraged, it stirs something in the self that responds immediately. It touches a well of truth and memory deep within us under the layers of defensiveness, and all the fears and pains of the past. At the moment when we are treated with respect, we are given an opportunity to remember our strength and our humanness, to which something in us responds, if not always consciously.

This is also what is being touched when we witness acts of bravery, fortitude or compassion—there is an answering response in us, because we are all capable of such things! I should go so far as to say that we could not recognize the greatness of these acts if we did not have their like within us, a thought I shall come back to later.

We can only appreciate and see what we can recognize, and if we recognize it then we must know it inside. There must be something in us that responds to beauty, love or wisdom. Something in you responds to the beauty, to the compassion, to the strength—it is not simply intellectual, or you would not feel it—it would not stir you. Therefore it is deeper than just the culture or the words, it is something in us. It follows that the more we focus on these positive aspects, the more we draw them out of ourselves—unveil them in ourselves and to ourselves.

At the moment of recognition and understanding we remember who we are: not perhaps outwardly with the mind, but our very core remembers. We identify with our truth, perhaps just for a flash, and for that time we are filled with renewed strength and courage; with hope and aspiration, and likewise faith for humanity.

New Light BEING WHAT YOU EXPERIENCE

If you can see beauty *then you are beautiful*.

If you can be aware of love, *then you are loving*.

If you can appreciate strength in the face of adversity, *you also have that strength*.

Remember something beautiful, or look at something you find beautiful. Focus on the feelings that stir within. Those feelings make you *beautiful*.

Think of something or someone you love. Focus on that feeling; it occurs because you are *a loving being*.

Think of an act of courage or strength you admire. Focus on the inner feeling it gives you. *In you it finds an echo*.

Seeing Ourselves as Basically Good

SO: you are basically good, just struggling with your defensiveness sometimes. How does that view of yourself feel? I imagine that you might feel that to think this is to condone your negative behaviour and that of others; maybe that it would make you morally lazy? Yet what are we saying if we think otherwise?

One of the things people most need is respect. The ways in which people go about getting and maintaining this vary, but we can all experience the feeling inside of wanting to stand up for ourselves and our rights as a way to achieve it. Many people I have counselled know the feeling of being treated as irrelevant or 'just a number', as if they do not

exist any more, or as if they are stupid or their feelings do
not matter. That feeling of hurt, or hurt pride, or anger can
be triggered in all of us, and from that defensiveness people
can react in dangerous, extreme and antisocial ways.

We can all react in this way, or at least feel the feelings. Our reactions may be controlled or contained, but
nevertheless, the body self rises up, and maybe that reaction comes out only in criticism of the other person, or
the condition—but if we are honest it is there in us all.
This need for self-respect ripples out into our environment as well, so that all people and areas that we love, and
in which we find safety, we also feel protective towards.

Imagine a terrorist. At one time he was a little boy,
maybe brought up to believe very strongly in a particular
religion. Perhaps that boy was also poor, and felt himself
treated as second class by others. He finds himself among
a group of people who feel that they and their religion
are so disregarded and disrespected that they are prepared
to fight and die to show that they and their God should
be respected. The understandable feelings of the boy, in
childhood and then in adulthood, and where he is placed
by society, are what drive him to acts of terror. His feelings of the need to be respected are something we all
have; his culture, or the extremity of his situation, leads
him in a direction that is itself extreme.

I was impressed by the scriptwriters of the American
series, 'The West Wing', which is about the well-meaning
President Bartlett. In a particular episode, the president is
about to give a major speech, when he hears that a terrorist
attack has killed American citizens. Changing his speech, he
acknowledges the pain to the families and the awfulness of

the event, but then adds that we should remember this about the terrorists: 'They were not born wanting to do that!'.

I believe that hurt or fear can lead us all into dangerous areas of defensiveness, but love and respect can lead us all into selflessness, true power and greatness. In reading I did for my work as a yoga teacher I came across the idea of the *siddhis*. These are 'magical' powers which arise and develop naturally as we gain control of our body, mind and emotions: such things as telepathy and the ability to lift objects with the mind. In a dream, I found myself doing just this. It was a tremendous feeling, but when I awoke I knew deeply that I would not want that ability in waking life because I could not be certain that I would not abuse it. In a situation where my defensiveness was very active, would I be strong enough or have enough emotional 'space' to trust I would not do harm with this ability?

I am suggesting that to believe in your innate goodness, far from being a lenient option, actually enables you to reconnect with the inherent integrity that you have. The following example is from a real news story. The subject was a special type of clinic where drug addicts were being rehabilitated through working with horses. One particular woman's story was very moving. No therapy had worked for her until the unconditional love of the horses helped her to love herself more—and as she did so, the horses in turn seemed to have more trust for her. She began to feel herself worthy of love, and that sense of being worthy of love, and of being able to generate love in other beings, is what was then helping her to stay 'clean'.

I often wonder if part of the large problem of reoffending among people in prison is the extent to which they have lost their self-respect—have lost the sense of being in any way 'good'—so that it then does not matter to them what they do. Perhaps they have given up on anyone seeing them as other than wicked, and so they continue to do what they at least get some recognition from—or some feeling of achievement and peer support—which is crime. The body self is attempting to find and maintain self-respect, wherever it can get it!

To believe in your innate goodness means that there is always a place that you respect to return to within yourself, no matter how defensive you have become. Although I have not counselled prisoners, I have counselled people who have committed acts they are ashamed of, and ones which have been extremely anti-social. When teaching I also dealt with many children who overstepped the mark! My experience is that the more you emphasize the innate goodness of a being under these circumstances, the more they respond with genuine remorse, instead of guilt; with a desire to let go of the defensiveness, to make reparation and to release whatever is inhibiting the natural flow of their goodness.

To say in effect, 'You are basically and innately good, just struggling with your defensiveness on these occasions', is both liberating and constructive. It allows a way forwards, and out of shame and impotence. It allows a return to innocence.

The Return to Innocence

THIS book could be called 'A Return to Innocence'— meaning a return to a place where we cease to hurt ourselves, through seeing ourselves in a new light. In doing so we cannot help but begin to see others in the same way. The terrorist becomes the little boy again, and this time he is loved, respected and nurtured. He feels safe and thus becomes a safe person for others to interact with.

One of the root meanings of innocence is not hurting. Getting back to a state of innocence is to find a state within where one does no harm either to oneself or to others, and thus where one feels no hurt. If we take the idea that hurt towards others arises out of feelings of hurt and fear within oneself, then to return to a state of innocence would mean a reconnection with the person side of the self and its innate goodness—*its wish to do no harm*.

Through an accumulation of guilt and defensive actions, innocence can be one of the things which adult earthly life lacks, which in turn causes so much distress. I am not thinking of the traditional concept of the loss of innocence in the Garden of Eden, but the innocence in all of us which can be covered over gradually as we get older. We may not even realize its loss at all, since so often we can feel that being adult is to be realistic and not show weakness. Spontaneity, childlike fun and appreciation of the small, beautiful things in life can be lost under a veil of what I can only describe as mild cynicism. This, of course, is a defensive reaction to the challenges of life.

Inwardly it is also possible to become very cynical about ourselves—to lose faith in our ability to be loving, kind and wise. Perhaps this is one of the reasons behind certain kinds of depression. We cry out for our own innocence; for belief in a world which is good, unlike the one in which we live which seems to be peopled by

New Light SELF-DOUBT

If this section resonates with you, when did you first think of yourself as 'bad'? When did it become a habit to doubt yourself, or feel you are always making mistakes? When did you lose the sense of anything being possible, and of life being an open book? The sense of 'badness', self-doubt, self-limitation are the kinds of inner thoughts I have found many people live with, and they are much more prevalent than we might think. There are plenty of people who seem from the outside to be capable, successful and strong, yet who are still plagued by feelings of inadequacy. There are those who are unaware that they feel 'bad', and yet much of their behaviour is based on defensiveness born of self-doubt. There may be particular areas of their lives to which this applies, which cause confusion for others, and anxiety in themselves.

Try this. How would it feel to believe that each time you awake you can be as an innocent child again—an experienced adult with the childlike sense of being open to all possibilities, without any self-mistrust? Innocence is more than self-belief, but is that quality of a child which causes us to look upon him or her

flawed individuals like ourselves. If we think in terms of innocence at all, there may be the sense that we can never go back—never find again those precious childhood times before we were aware of our protective ability to be harsh, unkind, cruel, critical?

I believe, and suggested in the previous section, that it is our loss of faith in ourselves through the concept of being thought 'bad' that produces many of the problems in our society and much of the sorrow.

with joy, and which opens our hearts to them. We can forgive their spontaneous acts of abandonment and energy, even when the acts cause mayhem, and it is that very spontaneity which speaks to us of the innocence beneath the actions. Can you remember smiling at a child's antics, even when they are producing turmoil? You may not condone the turmoil; you may make rules to limit it, but at the same time there is a freedom and joy in watching such lack of inhibition. When was the last time you looked at yourself in that way?

With the awareness that you are innately good, you can free your spontaneity and reconnect with a sense of joy in life. Awake each morning, knowing that even though yesterday you felt anger, mistrust, criticism—all of which are defensive reactions—because you are innately good, today can be different, and if it is not perfect either, then you are still learning how to believe in yourself enough to make it so. If by the end of the day you have slipped into those defensive places again, you need more self-belief, more faith in your goodness. Who is in the best place to give this to you, but yourself?

Make Sure you Feel Safe

BEFORE we move on to the next chapters, 'Dealing with Emotional Experiences', 'Mastering the Mind' and 'Liberating the Voice', I should like to come back to a statement I made earlier in the book, that the body self has the task of keeping us safe. Safety, as we know, does not just mean physical safety, but also emotional and mental safety, the feeling that you are worthy of respect, that you will not 'lose face', that you have a right to speak and can speak. It means that your feelings matter, that your intelligence and loveliness are without question because you are unique, and that they are certainly not dependent on your age, shape, size or education.

All that I have said so far in this book is, in effect, an attempt to help you create that safety within for yourself. I believe you feel safe when you know that you are learning, not failing; you feel safe when you know your defensiveness is only a protective mechanism, and that you are at the same time a person worthy of respect and love.

The safety is created through any of the feelings of self-respect and self-trust you can uncover. **Only when you have done that for yourself can you turn the spotlight on your defensiveness and release the pain that has caused it**. When you see yourself in this new light, it is at last safe to do this, and when you do it you will not add to the pain.

This is where, I would suggest, any confrontational counselling or psychology-based therapy could be ultimately destructive, even with the best of intentions. Any involvement where the recipient feels in a position of inferiority, and where they feel challenged, will be likely to produce a defensive reaction. Therefore to end this section I would like to add a few words that suggest guidelines for finding help in therapeutic situations, as well as reiterating the light in which I believe it would be most helpful to continue to read this book.

Choose Your Help Well

THERAPY is used in order to help us release our defen-

New Light INTERNAL SAFETY

Do you feel safe with yourself? Remember yourself as a baby or a young child. Feel your softness, your trust in those around you, your joy and excitement in everything. Feel what happens in your body when you connect with that sensation: the knots loosening, the tension dissolving, the need to hold yourself up around others gone. Feel yourself letting go. Are you a safe person for others to be with, now?

Can you, maybe a little at a time, keep the armour off when you are with others, so that they can see your innocence, your child? Can you take offence less readily? Can you be open, as a child, rather than manipulative? Can you be trusting before you are cynical?

Keep on practising reconnection with your innocent child, and gradually people around you will feel safe in your presence and enjoy your company. You will not appear weak or silly, but openminded and openhearted.

siveness and unveil our strengths, but I suggest we have to be careful that the therapy we use does not itself contain a punitive element, or a lack of belief in people's fundamental greatness, otherwise it will be counterproductive.

Look for the encouragement in all you read and listen to; look for those who help you to feel confident, not only in what you may some day be, but in who you are now. Look for those who support you when you inevitably fail (since that is the nature of learning) and do not feed your guilt. Look for those who consistently say, 'Yes, this is the strength which you will one day acknowledge as yours. This is how you will one day be on all levels of life, but

remember you are great now, and you are lovable in all your imperfection. Look for those who inspire and uplift you and help you to remember, but who also genuinely understand the way things happen.

Look for those who understand that failure is not always what it seems, that learning sometimes requires it, and that the imperfect journey is as important and as wonderful as the perfect end (if such ever exists!).

Look for those who do not tear down your walls before you have built up within the column of self-respect and love that will support your roof!*

*See the sections 'One to One', and 'As you are Now' (pp. 142, 92) for more on the kind of relationship which is helpful.

CHAPTER FOUR

DEALING WITH
EMOTIONAL EXPERIENCES

My hope is that through reading the next sections you will begin to rediscover the 'person self', and thus find a way to respect and live with all your feelings, because I believe that in that way your body self will begin to feel safe. Out of that sense of safety your control, trust and strength will be resurrected, will re-emerge.

I WONDER what you are feeling at this moment, and as you perhaps read the list of headings in this chapter? People have so often described how they feel to me in terms of guilt, fear, anger and depression particularly, and beneath them all, hurt. They often want to get a handle on their own emotions, and find ways of coping with those of others. What I have tried to offer here is a way of looking at these states which produce emotions in a way that I hope will allow them to be perceived differently. It seems to me that how you perceive your emotions adds to their impact, and seeing them for what they are can lessen their effects. My belief is that actually being aware of the process will help you, but I also offer some specific exercises to further this.

Having said that, our emotional states are as much in

need of respect as any other part of ourselves. They often indicate for us where we are hurting, so that we have a chance to do something about the cause of the pain; they can be protective or energizing, so that the point is not to overcome them, but to be able to deal with them from a position of trust and fearlessness. Trust is the key word here, because so often a person will tell me they cannot trust themselves when they react emotionally. The emotions can seem to spring up from nowhere, or linger on and on despite every effort, and are overwhelming at times. It can seem to the person as if they have very little control, and that the person self is completely subject to the defensive emotions. On the other hand, there are those who have found that their way to deal with hurt is to become extremely controlling of themselves, to the point where they believe they do not feel at all.

You may have noticed that in referring to the self that is not defensive I have begun to use the phrase, 'the person self'. It is the self that Harvey Jackins has referred to as the 're-emergent' human.* And it's the self that I discussed in Chapter Two, in the section 'Wrong?'—and earlier, in reference to Re-Evaluation Co-Counselling.

No matter how you perceive yourself, and whatever words are used, I should like you to feel you can trust yourself as you read on—even if your emotions are aroused, even if they never seem to be in control, even if you need to keep yourself tightly controlled. My hope is that through reading the next sections you will begin to rediscover the 'person self', and thus find a way to respect

*See Jackins, THE HUMAN SIDE OF HUMAN BEINGS (THE THEORY OF RE-EVALUATION COUNSELLING) in the book list.

and live with all your feelings, because I believe that in that way your body self will begin to feel safe. Out of that sense of safety your control, trust and strength will be resurrected, will re-emerge.

New Light THE CHILD

As you read, keep returning to your innocent child, just as you discovered that child a few pages back (p. 51). In therapy people are sometimes asked to remember themselves as a child at a particular age: how tall they were, for instance. I sometimes ask them to think of a child they know of the same age. This remembering puts people in touch with how it was—not through the lens of hindsight and adulthood, but though a simple reconnection with the experience of being a child.

Try doing this from time to time, as you read on.

Dispensing with Guilt

ONE OF the unhelpful effects of guilt is that it locks us into the past, not only into past events, but a self we have moved on from, even with just the recognition of something we wish we had not let happen. The past is a place we cannot change, and the more we re-enact it, the more entrenched, and possibly exaggerated, it may become. Bearing in mind that things are not what they seem, we may not be seeing things as they are in the present, let alone as they were in the past! And in addition, when you look back, you are looking at your past self with your present eyes.

The guilt we feel, even if it only relates to a short time ago, belongs to a past version of the self, one that lacks the experience you have gained in the meantime. There is a teacher who has said:

'Guilt is second judgment. It is looking at oneself with hindsight and saying, "I really ought not to have done that!". But, my very dears, if you really "ought not to have", you would not have.

'Know that at the moment of happening it was all appropriate. If you have learned since that the act is not what you would choose now, know that the act itself has brought you to this understanding. That was all it was meant to do.' *

This statement initially seems to excuse a lot, yet it fits with the contention of this book, which is that we only behave defensively—possibly causing pain to others in the process—because we ourselves are hurt or afraid, or our unresolved hurts or fears from the past are influencing our present perceptions.† The body self is behaving as it is programmed to do in trying to protect us. When we look back at the event we feel guilty about, we look with the eyes of the person self.

When we feel guilty we lose all sense of ourselves as innocent. From the hindsight perspective, we even forget things like how young we were when we committed some action, or the particular difficulties that caused us to behave in the way we feel guilty about. We can believe that we are not worthy of love, not strong enough to overcome the perceived negativity, powerless to affect change within ourselves and move on. There is even a way in which hanging on to the feelings of guilt makes us feel punished, as though that is something we deserve, or something which may strangely help us to feel better.

*EMMANUEL'S BOOK. See Appendix III, Books Mentioned or Recommended. †See 'Mindsets', in chapter five, p. 83.

Apart from the obvious damage to the self-esteem, any negative thoughts about the self will have a deleterious effect in many areas of the life. For example, far from helping us to make reparation, guilt typically has the reverse effect. When guilt arises there is a way in which the body self again responds defensively, so that—and you may recognize this—on the one hand you feel guilt and on the other you feel angry with the person or situation which makes you feel guilty. People have related to me how when they feel guilty they cannot face the person they feel they have hurt. On other occasions, people have said they have developed strong antipathy towards the person they feel they have hurt, so that this then becomes a justification for whatever it is that they feel guilty about. Family divisions based on these kinds of reactions can occur, and last many years.

Now that we have defined various guilt scenarios, the question is how to see things differently. You may not be able to change the events of the past, but you can influence the results of those events both in yourself and in others. The first step, however, is to dispense with guilt. The events of the past have an energy that traps you. Allow yourself to let them go and you will find your way forward.

If you wish to release a sense of guilt, fault, or shame, and return to a place of innocence so that you can move on, then what follows may help.

Moving forwards requires that we truly believe it is possible to do so. We have to be able to step firmly away from the inner world of past and future time, and embrace the outer moment innocently, so that we can do what needs to be done now.

New Light A DIFFERENT PICTURE

The first thing is to gain, or regain, a different picture of yourself. It is helpful to remember a time when you felt most loving and lovable. That you can remember this means it was never lost; it is still part of you, and will always be so—it is your person self. Picture this self strong in character and will, fearless and powerful, tenderhearted and wise—all that you know you are when you drop the veils hiding you from yourself and others. Imagine all sorts of situations in which you are demonstrating this inner self. What happens is that the more you focus on this part of yourself and allow the vibration of that image to colour your life, it will gradually become uppermost in all you say and do.

To aid this view of yourself, it will be helpful to look back at chapter two, and consider yourself as a 'work in progress'. In other words, review what mistakes actually are, and why they come about. To get back to innocence you need to trust yourself again. That trust is built on the understanding that even when you do not 'get it right' there is a way in which that is part of your learning.

I imagine that as you read these words there may arise in you thoughts of the pain that at one time or another you may have caused others which makes you feel guilty. It may seem as if you are dismissing that pain by thinking in terms of your learning process. Not so, you are finding a place within yourself where you can genuinely feel regret, rather than guilt. It is a place from which you can act to make amends if need be, without adding to a sense of your own unworthiness; a place where you can ask yourself what hurt or fear prompted your defensiveness in the first place, so that you can change your reactions in the future. In other words, it is a place where you do not arouse the defensive self, but allow the person self to be.

One of the ways in which guilt holds us imprisoned is through the perennial thoughts of the past that accompany it. The defensive self considers that perhaps by dwelling upon the events we might find a backdoor which will allow our shame to escape, but of course that never happens: we just dig a deeper pit of guilt, until time does the healing.

New Light CHANGING WHAT WE THINK

A way in which we can let go of guilt is to change what we think. One of the ways to do this is to replace one set of thoughts with another. When thoughts of your supposed 'wrongdoing' arise, practise letting them go as soon as you can and replacing them with thoughts of what you have learned from what happened, thoughts that can help you and others from now on. Here are some useful statements you might make to yourself:

'In order to learn and grow I shall generally make mistakes.'

'Whatever I think I have done, nothing will change it now.'

'In this moment I can make a difference.'

'I never lost my innocence.'

'I can control my thoughts.'

'Punishing myself will not help others.'

'I can trust myself.'

'I am strong in character and will.'

'I move on from the past with new understanding.'

'I am in control of my thoughts/my feelings.'

'My vibration is positive and helpful to others.'

Moving Forwards and Out of Guilt

ONE THING we have to be prepared for in people who feel hurt by us is their anger. The fear of someone's anger

New Light OPEN AND CENTRED

Openness is the way to show others who you really are inside—
it feels scary, but it is powerful. When your thoughts of 'wrongdoing' occur, and you feel shame, anger, despair, these feelings
will close you off from others. The sense of vulnerability and
shame give one the feeling of being almost naked, as if others
can see one's guilt, so the temptation is to hide, either physically
or through emotional coldness.

When this happens, move forwards towards others if you
can, even if only in your thoughts. Imagine giving them a hug,
saying something kind to them, asking them how they are. Try
to do the opposite of running away, whether that be physically
or just closing off emotionally. In this way you open the door to
mutual empathy and change.

is another thing that stops us from moving forwards to
say we are sorry, or to make amends. Anger is a natural
reaction. It arises when someone has felt vulnerable, hurt,
or afraid. You may have to deal with this once you move
towards the person you feel you have hurt.

Being prepared for this in your thoughts, and understanding that it is natural, may help you not to lash out
or run away in turn. See the other person's anger as the
means by which they can release their tension and get
back to their love—like an energy that is finding its way
out. Often the anger will not only be to do with you, no
matter what is said, but a chance for old anger to find its
way out too. Stand open to the winds of anger, and they
will blow themselves out.

> **New Light** AFFIRMING
>
> There is a way in which the repetition of a positive sentence can gradually have an effect on the body self. At first this will seem a useless exercise, because everything inside is shouting the opposite. What you are doing, however, is contradicting the old pattern or thought in order to reconnect with the part of you that is not defensive but centred and strong. An affirmation of your choice to walk away from anger, or to stand open to it without being cowed, will help release you from any sense of powerlessness or fear.

Dealing with our Anger

THIS SECTION is about changing our perception of anger, in order to release us from either guilt for or fear of this emotional release. If you can see anger as an energetic expression of the will to keep us safe, which is the role of the body self, then you go a long way towards being able to control it and use it appropriately, rather than it exploding unbidden. You also get a handle on this emotional response in others, which enables you to stay strong in yourself and not be buffeted by their feelings.

Remember a time when you felt angry. What anxiety, fear or hurt lay at its root? Did you feel

disrespected (hurt), >*overlooked*< (*fear*),
{misjudged} (hurt/fear),
undervalued (hurt/fear), <u>unloved</u> (hurt)?

It is my belief and that of Re-evaluation Co-Counselling that at the root of all anger (remember the little boy/terrorist) is a hurt or a fear—maybe a fear of losing something—such as position or credibility.

Anger is a way of expressing that hurt without showing our vulnerability. It is also a way of releasing the energy of the hurt and avoiding feeling a victim. Through
anger, we can feel as if we are doing something to change
the situation or others.

Sometimes, if we can find the hurt or the fear, and
release the pain of it in tears (for example), we find our
anger becomes more manageable or dissolves. When we
find the hurt we can also find ways of responding that do
not cause further damage. In other words, not only do we
have the option then of letting the anger go, but we have
the option of finding appropriate words or actions to deal
with what has caused the anger. The key words here are
'appropriate' and 'option'—for while anger is not understood as pain, it tends to find any means of expression
it can, and sometimes these means are not appropriate.
Then it can feel as if we are getting our feelings out, but
afterwards we tend to regret the moment. When anger is
not understood as pain it can seem that we have no other
options besides explosion.

What now follow are some ideas about how to deal
with anger. Sometimes anger manifests as frustration, or
as irritability or cynicism, but often it is aroused by the
feeling of not being respected, of being taken for granted,
treated as inferior or stupid, not loved as you should be,
misunderstood, not listened to, and many other ways too.
At such times the body self reacts as it does to physical
threat, and tries to defend itself with anger. But there is a
deeper problem here. When others seem to be disrespecting us, the tendency is to believe it—in some insecure, self-

doubting part of ourselves we believe we are not worthy of respect. It is this insecurity which makes the anger worse.

We cannot make others respect us. But we can respect ourselves. This is where standing up for yourself takes on a new meaning. Building up your own self-respect can help you get to the point where how others behave does not affect you in quite the same way—no matter how challenging they are. This building of self-respect can be done constantly, but is particularly necessary at the moment of anger.

New Light STRONG AND WORTHY OF LOVE

When you feel that flush of anger and aggression, try to find a moment to affirm to yourself inwardly that you are a 'strong', 'wise', 'loving' being (the words will vary here according to what is being challenged in you). Take a moment now to create for yourself an affirmation of your worthiness, one you can remember and repeat when you are next confronted by anger. This is standing up for yourself. The more you believe this, the less likely you are to be threatened by the opinions of others.

Although when we are angry it feels that we want others to change—to stop disrespecting us—in many ways it is within ourselves that we want the change to occur. We want to be free of our reactions to hurt, so that we can shrug it off, and so that we can sensibly and calmly decide how we want to proceed. One way to get to that point is to practise not expecting too much of others. I would also say, 'Do not expect too much of *yourself*'.

The two are linked, of course. Inside, we tend to be very self-punishing and self-blaming. The practice of forgiving the self, through understanding that we are still learning, means that we also do not expect too much of others. People are going to 'fail', in the same way as we seem to 'fail' and for the same reasons of fear and hurt. Seeing the anger as part of the defensive self of the person, and that their person self is still there as well, means you have more chance of speaking to the person self and allowing the defensive self to fizzle out. This is not dismissing the pain of the other person that is the root of their anger, but it does allow you more emotional space in which to console the hurt, rather than react to the anger.*

Even if what makes you angry is a direct hurt by someone, often that hurt is either not at all or incompletely to do with you. Sometimes people use situations to let out repressed anger and fear. Little things can cause out-of-proportion reactions because they remind us of other times and places, or because of other challenges which are happening in the life. Then that hurt/anger finds a release in the moment. This may also apply when you get angry yourself. **'This strong reaction may not be only to do with me'** is a good thought to have when confronted by antagonistically by someone. Similarly, it is a good thought to have about your own strong reactions.

Often when we feel angry or frustrated we are also, unsurprisingly, very tense! One way to help our minds, bodies and emotions is to try to soften, by relaxing, and thus release tension and rigidity, even if only physically. Practising deeper breathing is a wonderful tool to help with this. Often there are emotions of pain trying to burst

*See the section, 'One to One' in chapter eight for more about dealing with emotions in interpersonal relationships and in therapeutic situations.

out of us, especially at the throat (where we want to cry or rage), and in the tightening of the chest (where we feel the effort of holding our feelings in). Softening here physically can help us to cry rather than rage.

Much anger arises out of frustration, and frustration arises out of a feeling of being powerless. Being able to say how you feel may help to reconnect you with the feeling of being in control again. However, the wrong words can make you feel worse. You don't really want to hurt the other person: you think you do at the time, but you are more than just the defensive self, and the person you really are wishes no harm. **The right words are ones that assert your self-respect and also share your pain, without inflicting pain yourself.** Having the courage not to lash out, but to say how you are feeling instead, can feel like weakness, but it is a great strength and can diffuse a situation immensely: 'I am feeling really hurt at this moment', 'I am feeling very put down at this moment', 'I am struggling with feeling powerless at this moment'. All these statements give the other person the choice to see your humanity, to empathize and try to understand. As I suggest in the section 'One to One', you are appealing to the person rather than exacerbating the pattern.

There are ways in which we can use the immense energy of anger positively. When you feel angry, one technique is to think of all those people in the world who are feeling the same at that moment with understanding and love: this increases your compassion and tolerance. Another way is to use the energy in other activities, especially physical ones. TO GARDEN FEROCIOUSLY, sing with gusto, scrub with vigour, and WRITE WITH POWER

*See Appendix I for a 'Conscious Breathing' technique for every day.

can transform not only the garden, the music, the surfaces, or the piece of writing, but the energy itself—from destructive to creative. It may take a while, but it will happen because I believe it is the natural order of things. We are creative beings, and it is our natural disposition to create, not to destroy.

Fear and all its Sidekicks!

IN WRITING about fear I am also referring to all the fearful states such as anxiety, trepidation, nervousness and apprehension, as well as dread. Fear lies at the root of much of our defensiveness, and is a reaction that while useful in some ways, can also be inhibiting. Fear flicks the body self into protective mode, which can of course be appropriate. However, when a state of anxiety or nervousness becomes a chronic pattern, all kinds of behaviour can result which we may not want or find helpful. Yet again, it is possible that a person does not realize that fear is prompting their defensive reactions. Getting to know what your fears are, or when they are triggered, is helpful in releasing them.

People's fears are very real to them. Sometimes when we see someone in a state of anxiety the temptation is to be dismissive. '**Pull yourself together**' is a phrase which may lurk in our minds, even if we do not outwardly say it! And of course, we tend to see ourselves in this light too. So there is the pull towards guilt whenever we feel anxious or nervous about something. Feeling embarrassed about being afraid is a common reaction, one that I often witness in clients who are struggling with anxiety, phobia or dread. People say they feel they should be able to cope; they say they feel weak or silly; they say they should be strong, less sensitive, more courageous.

If you struggle with fears of any kind, including what you might at this moment feel are trivial anxieties, the thoughts overleaf may help you.

It seems to me that fear is such a primal feeling that it has the power to cause mental confusion, as well as physical constraint. You may have had the experience of being so afraid that you cannot move and you cannot think. That happens when we receive a sudden unpleasant shock that frightens us, but I have also counselled people who say that they live in a haze of mental uncertainty and self-imposed restriction because of their underlying state of anxiety, which feels ever-present.

New Light ACCEPTING YOUR FEARS

Acceptance of your fear is a great step towards letting it go. When you accept your fear you begin to take control of it—it is out in the open area of your consciousness, and begins to be seen for what it is. Even if you are only dealing with a relatively simple anxiety about an examination, for example, you might ask yourself the following questions:

'What are you most frightened of?'

'What do you feel is the worst *that can happen?'*

Simply acknowledging the answers to these questions helps to remove some of the miasma of dread that clouds the consciousness whenever we are afraid: a dread which is built up, in part, out of the not knowing.

Some major areas of fear are:

• Fear of injury, being hurt, degeneration, madness, or the death of oneself or others. This fear is obviously based on a need to preserve one's body and mind.

• Fear of appearing foolish, stupid, weak, unloving, egotistical, selfish, insignificant—in other words, fear of what others may think of you, or fear of upsetting others. This fear is based on a need to preserve one's self-esteem, pride and self-worth.

• Fear of losing control—exploding, weeping, screaming. This fear is based on the need to preserve one's sanity, and sense of self, and one's boundaries.

• Fear of not being able to cope.

• Fear of loss—money, people, possessions, physical and mental prowess.

• Fear of being taken over in some way—having no choice, being disempowered.

• Phobias.

The next few paragraphs, after 'Which Fear?', give some ideas about how we may tackle these fears, or at least those that relate to our interaction with life and other people.

New Light WHICH FEAR?

Finding what it is you fear to lose, perhaps using the list above, and then exploring your past for any patterns relating to this, may be a help in being able to feel better. The section 'Releasing the Pain from the Past' may be supportive in your doing this.

Trusting the Self

As you may see from the list on the previous page, nearly all fears are to do with a projected sense of loss. To lose something means that a situation or a relationship has changed and change is something that is harder to deal with in the future than it is when it happens. There is a way in which when the event happens the body self does cope much better than it thinks it will. Fear arises through projecting scenarios where we do not cope. Thus it is that I have found that **when people are afraid they are often not trusting themselves**.

Moving Towards the Fear

People feel that there is nothing they can do about a fear. A fearful state feels permanent, and the only recourse seems to be to move away, or to close off from the object of the fear, so having an action you can take is helpful. Actually to move towards and through the fear takes courage, support, confidence, trust—but the pay-off is tremendous.

Controlling the Mind

Many states of anxiety are based on what we are thinking. Thought is much more powerful than we sometimes realize, and our thoughts are often much more imaginative and larger than the reality. Hence the three-o'clock-in-the-morning scenario: when you are lying awake in bed, things can seem incredibly bleak! In the next chapter I deal with mastering the mind, but here I would like to say that in my experience it is the mind that controls fear in most cases except where there is a sudden imminent threat (sometimes known as the fight/flight reaction). However, what I am seeking to do in both this chapter (about the role of the mind in controlling fear) and the next (on mastering the mind), is to focus on the fact that

New Light   A GREATER VISION

One way to help yourself feel safe, empowered and trusting is to imagine something more than your defensive self being in control. Can you visualize your person self as you would like to be, powerful, aware and trusting of yourself? Take a few moments to get in touch with how that might feel. Imagine what you would do and how you would respond to life if that person self were always uppermost. Visualize yourself in a variety of situations in which you would normally feel anxious or afraid, and see yourself responding differently.

Focusing on this other part of yourself will also help if you are feeling negative about yourself in any way. Many negative thoughts about the self can occur in someone who is afraid. Being ruled by a fear means that you begin to doubt yourself, your contact with life and with others, to lack confidence generally in your abilities, strength, and decisions—in your worth. When and if this happens, to remember that you are more than you think you are is helpful. So too is remembering that courage is not the absence of fear. Indeed to feel afraid and still do what you fear takes great courage. Despite your fear, you are strong.

the mind operates on different levels. We can learn how to access mental states which are not subject to fear, and where we find peace, freedom and even joy!

It may be helpful to mention one of my personal encounters with this. Many years ago I quite suddenly found myself gripped by panic attacks, which started abruptly one day and continued for some months. I have described my panics as being like the moment when you think you are going to crash in a car, but instead of gradually fading with the cessation of danger, the feeling continues. At first I found that the only way to deal with the panics was to make myself go to sleep so that I no longer felt the fear! It is the feeling of not being able to face another moment of the fear which drives one to wish for unconsciousness, although I realize how fortunate I was in being able to achieve this sometimes, since often a sense of panic keeps one wide awake. I was abroad at the time, but when I returned to England I decided that I needed to find some means of controlling my mind—or rather, my thoughts, which I recognized as being the source of the fear. I saw that the feeling was in my mind, if I can put it that way, even though at the time I was not totally aware of what I was afraid of.

At that time, Transcendental Meditation was beginning to be well known in the UK, and was being used not only as a meditation technique, much like many of the thought-control techniques of today, such as Neuro-Linguistic Programming (though it is dissimilar in approach). I began to study and practise TM, where you are given an individual mantra to repeat for certain lengths of time during the day. Whether or not you believe in the spiritual aspects of TM, or the power of mantra, the fact of spending that time focused on a mantra, I found gave my mind something else to do other than be absorbed in fear thoughts. More crucially, it gave my mind practice in controlling thought, through focusing on one specific thought. Any meditation technique may have the same effect, particularly if it involves some mental focus, and having now practised Theravada Buddhist meditation, as well as creative visualization and yogic meditation, I can attest to the mental control that these practices can achieve, irrespective of any other effects.

Surrendering

Though it may seem ironic that I should do so, I should also like to offer the act of surrender as a way to let go of fear. This process of surrender is not resignation or giving in to the fear, but rather a way of feeling, paradoxically, more in control. It is a technique often practised in meditation, whereby you move towards and embrace that which you find difficult or fearful. One of the aspects of fear is that it seems to rob us of choice. Also, the fear itself induces more fear. With a process of surrender one takes the 'heat' out of the situation, if I can put it like that, such that the body self feels less threatened and less 'on high alert'. This can provide just the space necessary for the person self to gain control. Again, I offer this from personal experience, as well as knowing how it has helped others. If this is something which strikes a note with you, then you may like to follow the process given in Appendix I, also called 'Surrendering'.

Using the Breath

Some people recommend deeper breathing to deal with fear. This can certainly work for some people, yet others feel more fear as soon as they start to focus on their breath. Breathing is usually unconscious, but as soon as you make it conscious the mind can begin to think of what it would be like to be unable to breathe. When you are used to driving a car, the actions of depressing pedals and moving levers become automatic. If you start to think about them you find you fumble, and instead of relying on the automatic responses, your mind interferes and can inhibit the body's actions. Doubt—which is a form of anxiety—can get in the way of you being able to drive! Breathing is still a good option for most people, though, and I have included a useful breathing exercise in Appendix II.

I cannot repeat enough times how crucial it is not to feel despondent if at first these things do not work, and not to feel guilty if fear continues to be an issue for you. Fear is a powerful tool of the body self, perhaps its most powerful tool, and therefore relentless in its own defence.

Getting a Handle on Depression

IN THIS section, I suggest that there are a variety of ways in which depression can manifest. The fears of the body self can lie at the root of many depressed states, but it is important to make clear that there are forms of depression which have other causes, chemical or hormonal ones, for example.

As I have said, one of the ways in which fear can manifest, especially if it is chronic or unrecognized, is in depression. To be in an anxious state which seems to be without end and where one feels out of control can mean that the natural liveliness of the body is shut down. One can feel depressed on many levels: physically, mentally and emotionally, or be depressed without totally realizing what is happening. The body self cannot find a way to create safety except by shutting down—by adopting a constant state of prevention. We can recognize this in people who become agoraphobic, say, but we all have the possibility of such reactions in perhaps less dramatic ways.

Depression can manifest in a variety of ways. Those I have been witness to in counselling are:

- • lack of energy and will
- • lack of enthusiasm for life;
- • absence of spontaneity;
- • an inability to share or speak;
- • any feelings of being shut down;
- • extreme rigidity of thought, movement or feeling;
- • much time spent in passive entertainment;
- • hiding away from people and not joining in;
- • hopelessness;
- • long-term use of drugs;
- • lack of personal hygiene;
- • a seemingly uncaring attitude towards things and people.

I can imagine that just reading the above list could make anyone feel depressed! But many people experience any one of those things from time to time, without it meaning that they *are* depressed. But there are those who struggle with these states of mind and being for a long time. I have counselled people who feel one or many of the states on the list all the time, and it is a horrid place to be.

The causes of depression can be many, besides fear. I have worked with people who have traced their depression back to the shock of loss or bereavement, even if it was some time ago, an experience about which the feelings are still insufficiently unexpressed. Other causes might include

the end of a relationship, **physical exhaustion,** chronic guilt, repeated failure, *chronic lack of support,* mental and emotional confusion that seems to have no end,
lack of fresh air, sunshine or exercise.

The list also includes any major changes that have not really been adjusted to, chronic feelings of low self-worth, and an ongoing situation in the life that the person is finding intolerable, but is frightened to change.

Depression is often associated with hopelessness and despair brought about by chronic feelings, mental or physical states, or conditions, which the person feels have every possibility of continuing for a long time. So, too, it may link to feelings and thoughts about the self that have been exacerbated by events that have happened, and about which the person can do nothing, or thinks they can do nothing. As I have said, the body self becomes preventative, and the ultimate prevention is not to do anything, expect anything or wish for anything.

One of the first ways I would work with someone who feels depressed is to help them see their depression differently. As a mere reading of the preceding paragraphs can have a depressing effect, so too thinking of oneself as suffering from depression can be the same. The sense of hopelessness increases with the feeling that there is no hope of restoring control. However, I have noticed that if someone can gain an understanding of what the body self is actually doing to cause the depression, that person can at least begin to have faith in themselves again, so that control becomes a possibility.

If you are someone who feels depressed, and want to help the body self feel sufficiently safe to relax, then it is better to avoid telling yourself that you are depressive. Labels have a way of becoming grooves out of which it is hard to leap! Instead it may help if you recognize one or more of those signs of depression to seek ways of dealing with them, such as consciously releasing feelings around a bereavement or working to deal with locked-in guilt.*

*For another view of depression, see Sorrell, DEPRESSION AS A SPIRITUAL JOURNEY

It is also important to recognize that releasing feelings though raging or tears is quite different from depression.* Even though it may seem at first to add to your difficult feelings, it is important to recognize that exploration and release of your feelings about a bereavement, say, is healthy. For instance, the depression could be the result of locking yourself away from the pain, or refusing to acknowledge loss, which then becomes like a weight in the back of your awareness, one that pins you down and leaves you heavier still. If it is hard to get in touch with the tears, then try and address the fear that may be stopping you. It may be a fear of being out of control, of losing everything, a fear of pain, or a fear of making things worse. How many times have you had someone say to you, 'Don't hug me, or I'll cry!'?—not realizing, maybe, that the tears will bring the healing.

When you are feeling deeply depressed, it is hard to see that the thing you are going through will end, or that there has ever been anything different. It is like a physical pain, which when present is all-consuming. However, it can be helpful, especially when you are coming out of the tunnel and need some encouragement, to try and remember times in your life when things have seemed really bad, and yet you have come through them. Also, to focus on the enjoyment of anything new in your life or in life itself—springtime, new birth, or any possibilities for doing things which get your energy flowing either physically or mentally (any new project), or emotionally (any new feeling or sensation, or change of awareness). Being aware of new and different things may help you to see

*See the section, 'Other People's Tears', in chapter eight.

that life is full of possibilities. Just focusing on unexpected lovely things which happen, or remembering other times when something quite unexpected but good has come to you or to one of your family, again can present you with an image, if momentarily, that things are not stuck.

Other ways to do this, if they appeal to you, are to visualize situations in which you break free, and to feel the joy that can come with that freedom, or to find ways in which you can take small risks, make small decisions, do small things that are different (like breaking a routine) and gradually increasing these.

New Light   A NEW IMAGE AND A RELEASE

Here is a quick synopsis of the above:

•   first, get a different image of what depression is and how it comes about, which includes seeing yourself other than as a failure.

•   second, help yourself release the hurt from experiences which may lie at the root of the depression, remembering that tears are not the same as despair.

•   third, give the body self a sense that there is hope, energy and possibility for change, which will add to a feeling of safety and help it to relax any defence patterns that may now be inhibiting forward movement.

Using Sensitivity

YOU WILL have noticed that one of the themes of this book is the manner in which the body self copes with feeling unsafe, and how that leads to defensive behaviour and patterns. Some people who feel vulnerable react with aggression, others react with submission; yet more react with aloofness or cynicism. But all these reactions are merely ways that the body self finds to increase its safety.

Sometimes when we have had to deal with really harsh situations that have caused us pain, we might say we wish we didn't feel at all. Again this is only the body self's way of trying to decrease the feelings of hurt. My opinion from many years of listening to other people's pain is that ultimately most would not wish to decrease their sensitivity, but rather find ways of handling it better, or turning it to good use rather than having it overwhelm them.

When people talk to me about feeling vulnerable, I see it as positive, though it may not feel so, because the person is recognizing the lack of safety and acknowledging their sensitivity. From that position they can begin to see where the fears lie, and how they can turn the sensitivity to their advantage, rather than letting it defeat them. Of course, sensitivity is a word others may use in a critical way—'You are oversensitive'. In fact, being sensitive can increase our ability to relate and to bring about positive changes in our world. Your sensitivity then, arises out of keeping you safe, but this is not the only way in which it can be used.

The capacity of the body self to perceive threats, whether to mind, sense, status, body, self-esteem, or anything which affects its integrity, is excellent in many ways. It means that you have the ability to sense things, perceive things, make connections; to listen and to see with acuity. This ability can be increased and adapted for other purposes.

You may well have heard athletes or actors, for example, who when asked if they get nervous, say that they try to use the 'nerves' and let them stoke the adrenaline which is then used for their work. They also often say that

New Light SENSITIVE LANGUAGE

Consider these words which one could say all have a connection with being sensitive: *gentleness, meekness, vulnerability, receptivity, creativity*. Some of these qualities you may feel you would like to cultivate, and they come about through allowing your sensitivity.

Some, you may have a resistance to. If so, remember again the times when you have felt loving. At such times you might have agreed that *gentleness, meekness, vulnerability, receptivity and creativity* are all part of that loving self. However, at the same time, you may also remember that you felt strong, powerful, in control, confident and very real.

it is to do with rechanneling and control. In doing this they are redirecting the high anxiety energy that comes from fear of failure—the automatic body-self response. One might also say that they are using it, rather than being manipulated or overwhelmed by it.

This is not a technique available only to a few people who put themselves on the front line, but is something we can all learn to do, once we realize what is happening. These days, professional sportsmen and women have psychological trainers assigned to them who will help them use the 'reactions' to their fears, and make them 'responses'.

Your next question is going to be, **'How?'**! If I say that the simple fact of being aware that this process is going on will help, you will think I am dodging the question. However, there are legitimate reasons for saying this.

To be aware is to have a degree of detachment from the thing you are aware of—a little bit of space between the event and the reaction—a space in which you realize you have a choice. To be aware, in the sense I mean it, includes

all that has been said previously about learning and uniqueness, so that the awareness is just that: watching/seeing
without judging yourself negatively. '*Ah, so that's how I react
when...*'. I do not think I can emphasize enough how much
negative thoughts about our defensive reactions can inhibit
choice, creative response and change, and how much when
we recognize the truth of what is really happening, our
natural compassion and intelligence is released.

Having become aware/clear/understanding in this
way, you then know you have a choice as to what to do
with that reaction. You may let it go ahead, you may mod-
ify it, you may stop it, you may learn from it. There will
be no one right or wrong course; it will all depend on the
situation at the time, for you. This emotionally free space
allows the person you are to reassert him– or herself and
find new ways of responding, or ways to make things work.

There are other ways in which you can use the sensitivity
of the body self for good. You can deliberately foster it. By this
I mean you can focus on developing your listening and ob-
servation skills, developing your ability to keep your attention
on what is happening now to make you more efficient, developing your creative responses to all areas of life. The ability
of the body self to be single-minded, tenacious and observant
and to draw rapid conclusions can be harnessed in a constructive manner, as the athlete harnesses his or her fear. Again, this
is part of doing something deliberately, rather than being a
victim of your reactions. I've spoken before of my hesitation
in using the words 'conscious' and 'unconscious', simply because of the psychological connotations often associated with
them, but what you are doing is giving attention to an area of
yourself that would otherwise operate out of habit.

CHAPTER FIVE

MASTERING THE MIND

It is [the] ability to change the mind and to perceive things differently which will transform your life. It may not happen all at once, but having a handle on 'why' means you can see what is going on.

THE PURPOSE of this chapter is to explore some of the ways we use the mind in thinking and imaging, and how profoundly this can influence how we feel. Also, I wish to explore how multifaceted the mind can be—how we can be influenced not only by our immediate thoughts about what is happening now, but by deeper habits of thought which may not even belong to us!

I wonder what you are thinking at this moment?

It may be worth taking a few minutes at this point to focus on your thoughts, and all the different levels of them: surface thoughts connected with the moment, deeper thoughts connected with what is happening in your life more generally, and persistent thoughts. Perhaps, as you do this, you will also be aware of how much your thoughts are influencing your feelings, and vice versa.

New Light RELAXING THE DEFENSIVE SELF

Just allow the mind to wander. Let it go out of focus, as you can do with your eyes, and see what arises. With part of your mind, monitor those thoughts and the images that spring to mind. You might even jot them down. Obviously, if there is something deeply troubling you right now, your mind will be drawn back to it like a magnet, but most of the time you could be aware of a variety of thoughts, over which you may feel you have no control.

Focus on one positive thought, and see how, if you can keep the attention, that thought changes how you feel. The defensive self will be relaxing.

The Mind and the Feelings

THE MIND, or the thoughts at least, are often governed by how we feel, and how much importance we give to how we feel. When one examines it, a critical thought, for example, will be based on some feeling of hurt, pain, fear—some emotional response to the object of criticism, either in the present, or something which has built up over time.

For a number of years I practised as a Theravada (literally 'the Ancient Teaching') Buddhist. There is a question used in Buddhist tradition to promote mindfulness, which is: '**Who is it who feels?**'. It can serve to remind us that we are not just the defensive body self reacting to threats, but something more. The question promotes a degree of detachment that can reconnect you with your ability to choose. Using psychological terms as I have interpreted them, this practice is a way of using the mind in order to give you enough space to switch from a defensive reaction to a personal response. Those who practise mindfulness in this way can even get to the point where they have some control over physical pain, or at least remove the tension and fear surrounding it.

Mindsets

BESIDES our daily reactions to what happens in our lives, we also have what I would call 'mindsets': habitual ways of thinking that have come into being through some sensation—some reaction to feeling which then, like a pernicious weed putting roots deeper into the soil, has taken hold so firmly that we automatically think in those particular ways when things happen, or when we feel certain emotions. These thoughts may have begun life in the past—possibly in views picked up from the statements of the significant people around us in childhood—and have grown over the years.

It might be helpful at this point to explore a little the nature of perception. When I was working for a master's degree, part of which was on the nature of learning, I spent a good deal of time studying how we perceive things and what the mind does in order to translate that perception into thought and awareness. Since then, working with many people in counselling, I have been made aware again and again of how a person's mind interprets what the senses experience. One of the humorous examples I give when facilitating groups is that if you are going out with a man who has a red Porsche, you will have a tendency to see red Porsche cars everywhere; if that relationship ends and you start going out with a woman (yes, life can spring some surprises!) with a green Citroen, then you will begin to see green Citroen cars everywhere! The point is that there are a number of things which determine what we see—we select what we see, but also see what we are habitually conditioned to see, and sometimes we copy others in what we see.

There were a series of experiments carried out in the 1950s by someone called Solomon Asch: the Asch Conformity Experiments. They were designed to see if and under what circumstances people will conform to their group, against the evidence of their physical senses. The results were alarming even to Asch, who did not expect the degree of conformity that occurred.*

The point is that what we think is governed very much by what we feel. Many of those who conformed to the group opinion in the Asch experiment, despite their senses indicating otherwise, felt that to go against the majority would be to be seen to be different—obviously this was so uncomfortable as to influence them—or else they began to doubt themselves.

If such a situation as the wish to be part of a group can produce self-doubt and a skewing of reality, then how much more lacking in reliability will your experience of the world be if you have ongoing feelings about yourself which are negative—if you have feelings of low self-worth, feelings of shame, feelings of self-loathing? Those feelings may also mar your judgment, and certainly it is possible that your ability to think creatively

* You can read a summary of the experiment in Asch, S. E. (1951). 'Effects of group pressure upon the modification and distortion of judgment', in H. Guetzkow (ed.) GROUPS, LEADERSHIP AND MEN.

and intelligently will be impaired. Conversely, when you begin to change your view of yourself, then not only do you begin to feel better, but you begin to see more of the truth within a situation, and free your natural intelligence and creativity.

When we are seeking to master the mind we need to be aware of our mindsets so that we can choose whether they are enhancing, or whether they are getting in the way. Creativity of all kinds—and intelligence, as I have said, is the ability to think creatively—requires freedom from preconceived ideas or mindsets.

An example of holding on to mindsets is a conversation I had once with someone I know well. He showed a marked aggressive prejudice against a certain cultural group. I asked him if he knew anyone from such a group. He told me one of his mates at work was from such a group and added 'a nice bloke really'. I asked him why he was so dismissive of people from this cultural group when his colleague was a 'nice bloke'? He replied that it was what everyone said, and had said around him for many years, so it was what he said too, whether he really believed it or not. The Asch experiments sprang to mind!

We can have a tendency to hold on to our patterns of thought long after they have become redundant—not out of ill design or stubbornness, but because in their familiarity they have been our safety for many years. The skill is to recognize where those thoughts are coming from. Are these thoughts ones we hold now, or do they remain in our consciousness from situations in the past to which we no longer subscribe?'

New Light REVERSING OLD IDEAS

If you continue to practise the ideas of the previous 'New Light', and regularly 'relax the defensive self' over a period of time, you may find patterns of thought emerging: persistent thoughts about yourself, or your life, for example. Now, however, you can see them in a more detached way. You may wish to question whether you still truly believe these things. You may wish to change any negative ones to positive.

To understand another's point of view, and to be able fully to explain your own, it might be helpful to try thinking the reverse of some of your long-held ideas and see where that takes you. From what feelings do you think these thoughts arise?

Mindfulness is thus actively using the mind, rather than letting it be used by the emotions; mindfulness means that we take charge, rather than allowing ourselves to be ruled by the persistent and perennial mindsets we are accustomed to. Mastering our emotional reactions means to detach ourselves from an overprotective sense of self. Does it matter if we are hurt by someone's criticism of us? Who is hurt? Does it matter what people think of us? Do they really see who we are? Does it matter if people seem to misunderstand our motives or our actions, when we know? When the situations leading to these examples occur, it feels as if it matters a great deal, but if we are mindful we can ask such questions and more, and through that asking gain a wider perspective—begin to look with new eyes, and thus gain detachment from the defensive reactions of the body self.

It is worth sharing here a very funny (but stereotypical)

cartoon which I use frequently when facilitating groups on this kind of subject, not to point to the differences in men and women, but to what we choose to hear according to our feelings and thoughts. In the first picture a couple are having a romantic anniversary dinner. The man tells the woman how much he loves her and everything she does: '*You're so strong and capable. You look after the children so well, and work away from home. You're always there for me, even if you're a little bit moody sometimes. You're always smiling. You do everything so well. You are so creative and beautiful.*' At the end of his tribute the woman says: '**What do you mean, moody sometimes**?'. In the second image, a man and a woman are in their lounge. He is reading the paper. She is doing the ironing. She is saying: '*And you never put your socks away. I'm always having to tidy up after you. You constantly come home late and expect dinner to be perfect. You never make the bed, or clean the dishes after our meal. You don't pick up the kids or even go to their school events. You don't do the gardening, or wash the car*'. At the end of her diatribe the man says: '*Bed? Now?*'.

Whether we are men or women, what we see and hear is dependent on our inner process—that is, our underlying patterns of thought. For example, in the first cartoon image the woman's defence mechanism (and therefore her vulnerability) is so strong that her focus of attention is only on the one negative point among all the positive. She may hear the others, but she cannot take them on board, not at least until she's defended the negative statement. The strength of this defence could show an underlying propensity—a mindset—a way of perceiving herself through what she assumes others are thinking, which clouds her ability to hear or see anything different.

If you laughed with recognition at that cartoon, then I suspect you know that you too are capable of doing something like this. I certainly am! What we must try not do is blame ourselves—nor if possible anyone else—but seek for an understanding of why, and believe in our ability to change the way we think, no matter how entrenched it might be. It is that ability to change the mind and to perceive things differently which will transform your life. It may not happen all at once, but having a handle on 'why' means you can see what is going on. This is particularly valuable in our relationships with others, as you will read in various places in the section, 'Making Things Work'.

New Light WORKING TO CHANGE OUR PERCEPTION

If my comments on this cartoon speak to you, you may begin to develop this change of perception by making yourself aware of the daily slights and misunderstandings that can take up so much emotional space. Begin the practice of letting such things go as soon as they happen, by asking a question like: 'Who feels this?' You may like to set up a practice of beginning the day by reminding yourself that you are 'person', as well as defensive 'patterns'. It is good to remember that this exercise is to remind yourself that you are in control, not run by the actions or words of others.

The Power of Your Thought

LET ME describe something I watched on the television, which made me think again about the power of the mind.

It was a report of a medical experiment in which areas of the brain of a man who was quadriplegic were linked electronically to various household devices—like, for instance, the controls of a television. It had been found that with the right equipment, the man could manipulate matter—switch on the television for example—through just thinking about doing so. He said: 'I think it, and it happens' .

As I understand it, one of the aims of the experiment and ones like it is to re-empower those whose spinal chords are severely damaged, those people who can no longer move because the motor nerves can no longer receive messages from the brain. The hope is that they will, in the future, be able to do so by the direction of their thoughts. What a wonderfully liberating moment that will be!

This manipulation of the gross physical world by the power of thought alone leads me even more to emphasize this link between what you think of yourself and how you become. Think about being calm and peaceful, no matter the circumstances; think about being confident and open-hearted. By the same token, what about thoughts of being stupid, unattractive, weak, not good enough? Through these thoughts the body self gets a message which causes it to defend and contract, or to let go and trust.

Expectations

WHEN I read something like the 'New Light' above, especially if I have been practising these kind of exercises for some time, and still find things difficult, despite all the hard work, there is a tendency in me to irritation, guilt or despair. That brings me to another part of our thought

> **New Light** THE WILL
>
> For just a moment, think of one thing you do not like in yourself,
> or a quality you wish to change. It might be your poor timekeep-
> ing, say, or your short temper (no, these are just examples!).
> Imagine carefully the difference there would be if you were to be
> able creatively to affirm the positive. See that self, and affirm: 'I
> am ....'. Think as you would think if you were quadriplegic
> and had the chance to manipulate matter through the mental
> process I described; you would use your will in the greatest way
> you could, and your imagination. You would want it so much....
> That strong willing can, contrary to what we were taught once,
> have an effect on matter.

process which can be inhibiting, which is 'expectation'.

To change the habits of thought of a lifetime is a long
process! Yet, when we are in pain, of whatever kind, we
usually want to be rid of it straight away. So many books
are filled with suggestions which imply that in a short
space of time you will be different. But that is not always so, although occasionally changes can happen very
rapidly. I have heard Krishnamurti state vociferously: 'You
don't want it enough!', when people would say that nothing had changed. But to my mind, that kind of statement
is one of those which might only add to the defensiveness
of the body self, not make the person work any harder!

We have to ask ourselves why things take time, and why
harnessing our effort and our will to change is so hard,
rather than assuming we are lazy or vacillating. I like to think
of the example of an old-fashioned vinyl record which has
grooves. Our perennial thoughts have created grooves like

this, grooves that are very easy to stay in, and which can get deeper and deeper as time goes on. When we are seeking to change the thoughts that seem to control us it is like trying to flip the stylus up out of the deep groove. It may rise some way, and it may also slide back in—but eventually, if we persevere, the moment does come when we flip the stylus up and into another groove altogether.

New Light THE MOUNTAIN

Imagine your life as a journey up a cone-shaped mountain. The path spirals round and round. Down the mountainsides there are a number of streams: a stream of dealing with anger, a stream of having difficulties with a parent, a stream of fear, a stream of unrequited love, a stream of guilt, and so on. As the path spirals round, it inevitably crosses each of the streams again and again. However, as you are travelling upwards, the crossing is at a higher level of the spiral each time. It can feel as if it is the same stream, but it is always different. Also, you will have learned something about the stream from all the previous crossings (though you may not always realize this) and you have changed and moved on.

The trouble, of course, is that every time we slide back into the groove we tend to think we have failed. We measure ourselves against the end product rather than seeing the process. The athlete has to practice many times before he pushes his performance further. To have a vision of how you want to be at the end of the process is helpful, but when you are constantly knocked back into your old defensive self, it is even harder not to be disheartened. Don't do too much comparing! As we have seen, any negative thoughts about the self are not going to help the change, but just succeed in stimulating the body self to more efforts at protection in the old way! This effort to protect yourself may mean giving up, or switching to another type of exercise, and will certainly not help the self-respect.

There has to be a way of setting the will to change, letting expectations go, and glorying in the process. A member of a group I once ran said something very helpful: 'It's the step back that helps you know where you want to be'.

As You Are Now

JUST the simple fact that you are reading this book probably means that you are in some way wanting to 'see yourself in a new light'. But in my experience, the first step in so doing is to celebrate and affirm yourself as you are now. For me this is the foundation of good counselling practice precisely because it releases the body self from its defensiveness; there is no need to defend if you feel no attack. Once someone feels safe and respected, and particularly feels they are worthy of respect, then those parts of the self which inhibit our ability to change become less dominant, and the 'person' can begin to emerge. In my experience with people I have counselled, to change once we feel safe in the present is an almost instant thing, and immediately visible in the demeanour of the person in front of me.

All that I have so far said about the process of learning and unavoidable failure, as well as about the 'pattern and the person', can lead to a change of vision about who you are right now. To be able to say: 'Ah, now I know why, and it's not because I'm bad, stupid, lazy, etc.', means your defences are down and your self-esteem can rise. Believing these things—taking the heat out of failure and understanding why it happens—can of itself bring about change. Then any exercises you do, like the 'new light' ones in this book, can really begin to work because the process is understood.

You might think that when your expectations are lessened you will become complacent and that some of the drive—the will—is removed. An example of how this is not the case comes from my own experience comes from my years of experience of professional singing training, though this is by no means the only story I could relate. My teacher is, I consider, one of the best, and one of the best at exemplifying the above philosophy. She has the immense skill of celebrating where a person is in any moment of time, and using where that is to move forwards. Her skill is in an intuitive understanding of just this need to avoid arousing the defensive self, and instead to encourage self-belief. She has an awareness of the self-doubting emotions that can arise when one is developing the voice—and this is particularly true with the voice* —and she makes sure that every step of the way one feels respected, not chastised or bullied.

What this kind of skill does is to keep me at the most constructive point of learning while avoiding, wherever possible, the pit of failure. It does not mean that there is any falseness in what she says, because she understands that to be perfect is not about some ideal, but about how she approaches the moment and uses it in full. She understands that with this kind of respect for you as you

*See p. 106 in the chapter, 'Liberating the Voice'

are now there comes a liberation of all your will, effort, energy, self-belief and skill, which will takes you on to the next stage of learning and so on.

The expectation, if any, is that you will progress simply because self-doubt is removed and all the body self energy is therefore used to fulfil potential, rather than in preserving self-esteem. It is my experience that when this happens, you can look with confidence, for yourself, at the things you need to change, and find the means to do it.

Allowing Self-Confidence

YOU MAY initially wonder why I have included self-confidence in this section about the mind. The reason is that how we think about ourselves, particularly in relationship to others, often allows or does not allow us to feel confident.

Think for a moment of the people around you and those you know. How do you feel you measure up to them? My suspicion is that for most of us there will be quite a few whom we feel we do not measure up to, whether in one area or in several. There will also be some we feel we are better than, and there might be a tendency in us to criticize these people for not being good enough. This tendency comes out of the defensive self trying to help us feel more in control. I sometimes call it putting others down so that we can put ourselves up. In either case it is not a weakness in us, but a defence.

The amount of confidence we then feel is often dependent on how we think we measure up. Making comparisons can either produce insecurity or the tendency to criticize.

In fact, many more people than one would think lack

confidence in themselves. How someone appears is often in contrast with how they feel and are in their inner self. Self-confidence, or self-belief, is something many struggle with inwardly, if not outwardly—and the level of it can be a mindset, rather than a temporary reaction to circumstance. From the outside some people can look and seem very confident but, as I've said, this outward persona can hide a very different person underneath, who perhaps feels just as tentative, vulnerable, sensitive and unsure as anyone.

There are all kinds of other ways in which our self-confidence can be battered, again mostly through comparison with others: through schooling, through difficulties in relationships at home and work, through media and advertising, through what we think of as our failures.

On what is your self-confidence or lack of it based?

- What others think of you?
- How close you come to a particular media image?
- How many exams you have passed?
- How many mistakes you have made, or not made?
- What significant people in your childhood or at school told you?
- Whether you have a 'good job' and earn a lot of money?
- Who you know?
- Where you have travelled or what you have read?
- Where you live?
- Whether you are in a relationship?
- Whether you have children?
- What your parents do?
- What your voice or skin is like?
- Howwellyoufitinwithyourfriends,orwhatfriendsyouhave?

- What interests or skills you have?
- How much praise you get? How you compare with others?

You will notice in most of the above a kind of confidence based on comparison. Through asking those questions the las thing I want to do is add to any negative feelings about yourself, but rather to point out what happens in the sort of society in which we live. It is not easy for anyone to develop a confidence in themselves based only on their internal sense of worth. The school system in England, and I suspect elsewhere in the world, is such that people are praised for their achievements relative to others, to the point where even the schools themselves are valued according to how well the students perform in examinations, rather than how well each individual child fulfils its own potential. This means that the vast majority of students are daily confronted with failure or mediocrity, according to social custom. How does anyone end up with any sense of confidence without making a judgment of themselves in comparison to others?

One of the ideas that can get in the way of being confident is the idea that self-effacement is the way to humility. In my experience the reverse is true. When self-belief is strong it does not result in arrogance (arrogance accrues from the opposite of self-belief); rather, it enables us to go forward and meet others and to stand in our own strength without shouting about it.

All aspects of relationships are about flowing outwards from ourselves towards life, but it is hard to flow outwards towards others and to life—or to stand still in your own strength—if you doubt yourself, or feel weak or lacking inside. It is that lack of confidence which makes us hold things to ourselves and stifle spontaneous expressions of kindness, praise or love towards others. It is also that lack of belief which makes us demand outwardly that people see how good we really are. So the braggart is someone who says with their defensive behaviour: 'Hey, look at me. I am good. I am clever. I'll show you!' The person who really needs to believe this is the braggart him or herself. **It is not an excess of self-belief which gets in the way of humility, but a lack of self-confidence**.

In the first section I talked about the integrity of the self. What a belief in your uniqueness does is to show you a different way of perceiving yourself, through a unique set of eyes, which are yours! Not only that, but a unique set of eyes which have lost the false lenses of self-disparagement. It is not that you put on rose-tinted spectacles instead, but that you understand that you cannot be compared with anyone, and therefore you regain your integrity. In losing that wish to compare, you realize your confidence is based on an inner sense of self-belief, not any outward evaluation.

The more we feel supported within the more we can be tolerant without. Ideally we need to internalize all those outward expressions of support. We need to change our views of what matters and of what confidence is actually based upon. It does not matter what relationship you feel disadvantaged in. Even if it's your boss, for example, and even if she could sack you on a whim, she has no authority over you as a person. No person is truly more powerful or worthy of respect or of listening to than you are.

New Light A CONFIDENCE PROCESS

If lack of confidence is an issue for you, take some time to think about your various relationships in the following ways. Ask yourself: 'Do I feel a lack of support from others? Do I feel angry or hurt because others do not agree with me, or seem to be against what I want to do or what I say? Do I find myself seeking to make people be like me, or think like me? Do I feel unsupported and alone? And finally therefore, 'Am I giving myself enough support through thinking positively about myself?'.

Imagine all the people you know gathered in a room and facing you. The group includes all those people whom you feel you do not measure up to. Imagine yourself standing before them, knowing that in your uniqueness you are as powerful as they are. Lack of confidence produces feelings of inadequacy and a sense that everyone else has more authority than you and hence more power. Draw yourself up erect, looking into the eyes of each one of these people. Smile and relax. Feel that you can listen to them without feeling threatened; that you can speak without fear or anger, even when you disagree.

Imagine different scenarios where you can go through such a routine with these people. Self-confidence is the degree to which you truly believe you are as powerful and have as much authority as anyone else. Feel that even if your words are dismissed, as I imagine they may be in your mind, it is the ability to state clearly and to feel confident in yourself which matters.

You may have to practise this a few times in your mind before this takes root, but eventually you might find you can practise it in reality. When next you are in a group of people, go through the inner process above and see whether it changes how you feel.

More Confident Than You Think

THERE are ways in which you may have more confidence than you think. We do not always notice things about ourselves, and you may have had the experience of someone meeting you after a long absence and telling you how much you have changed. You may have been surprised, because you spend all your time living with yourself and had not noticed! Familiarity with oneself hides many of the changes that occur gradually. In a similar way, the insecurities and anxieties you may live with all the time can hide your strengths from you.

The RC paradigm mentioned at the beginning—the 'pattern and the person'—demonstrates this duality, which means that simply because you have insecurities you do not necessarily lack a strong sense of your worth. It may be buried much of the time, but your self-worth does resurrect itself when you are under attack. The aim is to bring your sense of self-worth or confidence into 'conscious' awareness—to bring it more fully to the fore, shall we say?—so that you call on it in place of your defences, and the sense of being able to be threatened diminishes.

If you are the kind of person who feels lacking in confidence, examine your feelings right now, after reading the previous paragraph. Might there be some inner part of you crying out that it is worthy of respect? Or some part of you saying it has every right to feel confident because it is powerful, intelligent, creative, good? If so, I would say that that part is your unique person, underneath all the received patterns of the past and the hurts.

This means that we have consciously to question our

view of ourselves whenever it is a negative one. We have to look and look again, to make sure that we are seeing what is really there, and not what we have been told, or even told ourselves in a moment of doubt. We have to listen to make sure we are hearing our true voice, and not the voices of other people in our past who, out of their own defensiveness and hurt, have told us we are something we are not. In constantly questioning this negativity you regain your confidence, and in so doing you open up the possibilities for all kinds of changes to take place.

Let us return to the analogy of the athlete—or, if you prefer, the musician at the beginning of the book. Even those who are at the height of their profession will tell you there is no perfection, only a continuing effort to improve. Set that scale against your own life, in whatever area you lack confidence. If an athlete or a musician did not believe in themselves they would not be able to get anywhere. Their lack of self-belief would pull them down at every step. With every race lost, every phrase played badly, they would want to give up.

Could it be that a lack of self-belief (or whatever it is that you feel in yourself that makes you doubt), is hampering your development and keeping you from your potential? If so, you have a choice to see yourself differently, but the patterns may well be very strong.

One last thing, though. You may have said a forceful 'yes' to the question above, and then added (possibly with a degree of frustration!), 'But I can't seem to believe any differently about myself'. This is precisely where it might be helpful to explore the past a little more in order and so free your confidence to move forwards.

Releasing the Pain from the Past

OUR EMOTIONS are often influenced by what we think and the persistent view we have of ourselves. This is particularly true of the degree to which we are aware of our self-confidence or otherwise, for all the reasons mentioned. Much of this lack of faith in the self can be linked to actual events in the past, which have produced emotional reactions and fostered this self-doubt. Although these events may not be happening any longer, the emotions can be 're-stimulated', as RC calls the process, by events in the present. Once self-doubt is there, it can gather moss like the proverbial rolling stone, with further incidents adding to the conclusions about the self, until it becomes a perennial thought.

As many readers will know there are a number of schools of counselling and psychotherapy that encourage the person to explore their past in order to facilitate change. This is certainly true of Re-Evaluation Co-Counselling, but in this case for a specific purpose. The aim is to release the locked-in emotions from the time of trauma or difficulty. I liken this to removing a veil of emotion which has clouded the present, so that the intelligent, confident, beautiful person is revealed to the person themselves. The important thing is that the unreleased emotion keeps the human being stuck in a reactionary groove, and with release there is the opportunity to see the world from a new perspective.

When you begin to look at yourself with new eyes, and contemplate the walls you may have erected around yourself, you will start to understand why you react to things in the way you do. This will involve exploring your past, even if only the most recent phase. It does not really matter where you begin, because there may well be patterns of defensiveness that will manifest in a variety of circumstances—the present can lead you backwards and the past can lead you to how you reacted only yesterday.

As I have said, the patterns of defensiveness linked to the past can be triggered by events and people in the present. In this way you can see how someone who felt consistently inadequate before a parent or teacher, to the point of developing feelings of hurt that then got locked in place, may well have the same reaction when faced with another kind of authority figure in adulthood, no matter how different that authority figure might be.

It is this kind of persistent reaction which exploration of the past is designed to explain and release. To this end, one of the techniques we employed in RC, when first working with a new person, was to say if that person reminded you of someone in your past. The understanding was that if you made yourself aware of the similarities of body, voice, dress, etc., you would be able to avoid some of the resulting re-stimulation.* You would then be able truly to listen to the person you were with in the one-to-one session.

One of the things which I have found can happen in counselling is that the person may have a resistance to looking at past events because they instinctively resist being in a situation where they feel they might be blaming others—their parents, teachers or whoever. The point of

---

* Again, I use the word in its technical sense, re-stimulation being the word used for when a feeling is triggered in the present which is to do with an event in the past.

the reviewing, however, is not to blame, but to release tears, fears, and rage, so that the incidents no longer have the power to hurt.

If you decide to look at past events that have caused you pain, keep in mind the idea that those who hurt you were also reacting defensively. That enables you to let go of blame, but it does not mean you cannot rage and speak out in order to release your feelings and your voice. Many people relate to me how, as a child, they felt that either they themselves were unheard or else their pain was.* The knowledge that you are releasing pressure and re-leasing your self, rather than simply lashing out in blame and punishment, is helpful, not only because your loving self will not really want to cause hurt, but because simply blaming keeps us locked in the pain.

I think I need to repeat that looking into the past also needs to be done with as complete a respect for your-self as you can possibly feel. An RC counsellor will listen with total respect for the person, no matter what is said, for all the reasons I have mentioned throughout the book so far. An RC phrase has it that in the sessions there are 'two intelligences working together.' When you are ex-ploring your own patterns this is the kind of approach you need to have towards yourself. Without it, you will be in danger of falling into guilt, shame, comparisons, re-gret, hopelessness, self-recrimination, as well as dwelling critically on past hurts. And when you can look at yourself with love, you will have more chance to look at others in

*See the next chapter, on 'Liberating the Voice', and in particular the section 'One to One', which offers more to do with being heard and how we can both listen and express ourselves fully

the same way, even those who may have hurt you.

It is worth offering here an easily-remembered sentence which somewhat parallels a quotation earlier in this book, 'If you could have done it differently, you would have done it differently'.* You may like to reiterate, too, that **those things we think of as being our greatest weaknesses can, with awareness and release, be turned round and become our greatest strengths**.

New Light REVISITING DIFFICULT MOMENTS

Begin by recalling an event in the recent past which produced feelings of lack of self-worth, confusion, frustration, or perhaps a feeling of being stupid or ignored. When in your life did you first feel like that?

Revisit that time in your mind and try to be there as the confident inner self you know yourself to be. Speak your mind. Do what you need to do to feel understood and safe. Contradict any negative statements about yourself. As in the New Light headed 'A Confidence Process' (p. 98), stand tall and erect. Be calm. If you are very young, bring the protecting influence of your adult self into the scene before you. Allow the hurt to flow in tears or rage if you need to, knowing that, as you do so, you are returning yourself to a state of balance.

You can continue to do this with other similar incidents in your life, but you may not need to go through all the cases of re-stimulation. However, you may find that you want to visit this earliest event again.

---

*See the quotation from the teacher Emmanuel on p. 56.

CHAPTER SIX

LIBERATING THE VOICE

Being able to voice your inner feelings, whether that is in singing or any other kind of verbal communication, is a powerful way of regaining your integrity, strength and confidence.

IN THE section of chapter eight called 'One to One', I have given some suggestions about how to foster communication in order to make things work, but here I would like to address the issues around reconnecting with your own voice, for the reasons mentioned in the last section.

Alongside the singing training I've received, I've been running workshops and retreats with such titles as 'Sound your Own Note' and 'Experience your Own Uniqueness'. The courses are not about singing as such, but are rather wider in scope. What I have discovered both personally and professionally is that being able to voice your inner feelings, whether in singing or in any other kind of verbal communication, is a powerful way of regaining your integrity, strength and confidence. It is also something many people find very hard to do, because they are frightened of it and feel embarrassed about it.

Given the way in which we are educated, I do not find this surprising. It is precisely the pattern that Susan Boyle, the singer, encountered. She was one moment a subject of ridicule and then—once the public suddenly heard her voice—welcomed with joy and feted like no one else. She did not 'look the part', but when she sang so beautifully, I believe people were saying in their hearts: 'Yes, yes, yes, that is me; that is what we all can do if we are allowed and encouraged! She speaks or indeed sings for me, and all of us who have ever felt throttled!'

Of course, I am not seeking to confine these arguments to singing, but referring to all ways in which we feel we do, or do not, have a voice. People so often feel stopped from speaking, unheard, misunderstood, or feel that are unable to find the right words. In counselling, part of the work the person and I often do together is to help someone who feels blocked to rediscover their own 'voice', in whatever way they feel is appropriate.

Possibly more than anything else, liberating our voice releases inhibitions and strengthens our self-confidence. We are a highly verbal society, whether cheering on our team at a football match, singing in the bath, or talking with friends. Today some of the prejudices around what a 'proper' accent is have been broken down, but we are still offered very little training in verbal communication. I am not thinking of how to debate, or public speaking, so much as help in discovering how to communicate effectively. It is done not by becoming someone else, but by finding your own voice and expressing your own self through it. We return again to the confidence gained by believing in our uniqueness, as opposed to comparison with others, and to the nature of truth.*

*See the section, 'What is True?', in chapter eight, below

When you voice something, or sing, you do at least two things. One is that you reach out to meet others and the other is that you give something of yourself. You show something of what your inner self is like, whether it is showing your emotions (through your tone of voice), or what you are thinking (through the way you use words). This is why the experience of speaking is such a threatening one for many, for it puts the self on show.

One of the most powerful ways of disconcerting someone is to remain silent when a response is expected. Some people use silence as a defence in the 'negative' sense, but there is also the saying that he or she is wisest who speaks least. That sort of silence is eloquent in itself. Others will be silent because they fear to show what they are thinking or feeling, or because they cannot find adequate words to express how they feel. Yet they often have a longing to speak. People have said to me, 'I just couldn't find the words when it happened, but afterwards I thought of all the things I could have said, and I'm fed up I couldn't say them at the time!'

Before they have been conditioned, children will talk and sing without inhibition. It is a natural part of living, this wish to express the self. When we are adults, to be able to reconnect with childhood innocence is a very liberating thing.

Talking

DURING counselling, people have described to me a number of ways in which they feel verbally inhibited. Some feel they have nothing important enough to say, while others admit they are frightened they will say something wrong. People will say that they don't feel important enough to contribute, or are not confident enough. Some people add that when they do speak it comes out inappropriately. Many people will tell me that they do not like the sound of their own voice, especially when they hear it on an answering machine or some other low-fidelity recording device.

Those statements point to the confidence that can be harnessed as well as the insecurity. To return to my earlier argument, they show that there is a way in which inside we feel differently from how we appear. It may feel like stating the obvious, but this is particularly true for many people who may are seen as 'old'. They tell me that they do not feel any different inside, and it is deeply saddening that others seem—or society as a whole seems—to think of them in a different way, simply because their body has changed its appearance.

We hear our own voice in a different way from how it sounds, because inside ourselves it is connected with all the levels of being, both the patterns and the person. What gets in the way of complete or appropriate expression is that the person finds it difficult to articulate all the different levels of emotion and thought at once. The work we do in counselling is to help the person find a lucidity—to explore all that they are feeling and thinking, and realize the complexity of their being. Far from making them feel split or a multiple personality, what this exploration does is to help the person understand where the confusion may come from, and assist them in deciding how to articulate what they really want to say.

Incoherence is a good word to describe not only the inability to speak clearly but the feeling of not being consistent—of having all sorts of feelings and thoughts which seem jumbled or contradictory. An exploration of one's inner world shows how this is part of being human, and where the contradictions can arise through the way in which we defend ourselves and veil ourselves. Coherence comes from understanding the process.

New Light VOICING IT

Is there something you are longing to say? Picture the scene in your mind. Imagine you have shed all inhibitions and can voice all that you wish. If you are facing someone shortly, imagine countering all their responses with your own. (It may be helpful to write down all the levels of what you want to say as you do this, so that you can use the words later). Feel erect, tall, in command and fearless.

As you read the word 'fearless' perhaps it triggered in you what it is that makes you afraid to speak out in this particular context (and maybe others)?

As a subsidiary part of this exercise, you may ask yourself when you first felt this way, and go through the process of releasing the pain of the past and contradicting any negative statements about yourself.

Armed with the words and the rediscovered confidence, you may find it easier to face the other person for real.

What Do you Say about Yourself?

HAVE you ever discovered that there are ways in which you persistently use descriptions of yourself that are not positive?

To demonstrate this, let's contemplate the difference between two scenarios. In the first, Joanna is getting older
and the skin on her face is beginning to sag. She doesn't like
this at all, and tries many options to change her appearance,
eventually giving up, but also describing herself as 'vain'.
Now Jemma is also getting older and the skin on her face
is beginning to sag too. She doesn't like this at all, but asks
herself why? She discovers that she has bought into the idea
that young and firm skin is beautiful and the opposite is
not. She stops trying to make her skin better, but seeks ways
to affirm that beauty is not dependent on age.

The point of this example is not merely to do with
how we can have a tendency to accept cultural images
of ourselves, but about the depth of mistrust that we can
have about ourselves, without necessarily realizing it.
Joanna, just as much as Jemma, is trying to move beyond
the cultural image of herself, but her way of doing it is to
berate herself for 'failure'.

There is a fundamental difference between the two approaches, which will have many knock-on effects. Joanna
calls herself vain, but at what cost to her self-esteem? Not
only does calling herself vain fail to offer any solutions, it
adds a layer of criticism to someone who already feels not
good enough. In effect, it adds a level of sagging skin to
the one already there! If I were in a counselling relationship with Joanna, I would be seeking to help her let go
of that punitive view of herself and find another way to
understand what is happening.*

The problem is that often, in my experience, we do

*See the section 'One to One' in chapter eight (p. 142) for an example
of how one might do this.

not realize how we are using language, what it signifies and what it does to us. For one thing, language entrenches thought. Continually to repeat that you are vain, or ugly, stupid or weak teaches the body self that it is so. At the same time, that same body self is protective, so we are setting up a conflict within. On the one hand we are damaging our own self-esteem, and on the other hand we are rising to defend ourselves.

In counselling work I have witnessed this conflict on many occasions. For example, someone is disparaging about their intelligence—they think of themselves as stupid—but the body self becomes aggressive when their associates seem to be saying the same thing. No matter how much the person deals with their reaction to their associates, until they stop thinking of themselves as stupid, situations will keep occurring which seem to confirm it.

The language we use without thinking is frequently indicative of our mindsets. Words used casually demonstrate habits of thought. They can also be words we have adopted from what others have said about us. I sometimes ask a person: *'Where did you first hear that?'*. It can often turn out to be from someone in their early life. Our choice of words indicates how we feel about ourselves much of the time, but so too can the use of language to create pictures. People will often use symbolic images without realizing it. Possibly it is easier to talk in this way, especially when it is hard to put one's feelings into words. For example, '**I feel like I've come up against a brick wall**'. On one occasion during a counselling session when this was said to me quite casually, we explored what the brick wall felt like, what it symbolized for the person, and eventually what lay behind it—all of which was helpfully revealing.

I listened to a radio programme some time ago, in which a well-known American child psychologist was recounting a story of how she had helped a child back to health. The boy had no language skills and was hyperactive and aggressive. His parents had taken him to many doctors and therapists to determine why and to find a cure, without success. The child psychologist on the programme had the child in her playroom, which contained all kinds of toys, and simply watched him. One session, he picked up a crayon, got some pieces of paper and started to draw two parallel lines across the paper. He then grabbed another sheet and did the same thing. The lines curved and wiggled across the paper, and when he got to the edge the child would take another piece of paper and do the same thing. At the end of the session, when the child had gone, the psychologist was left with a sheaf of papers, all with two lines running across them. She was, understandably puzzled, but laid the pieces out on the floor, to see if there was any pattern. A thought came to her—lining the papers up end to end, the two lines on each piece seemed to join up. She phoned the boy's parents and asked them if the child had been tested for tapeworm? The result, when he was tested, was that the boy indeed had a tapeworm inside him, and his behaviour was a result of the irritation it produced in his whole system. The tapeworm was removed and the boy's behaviour normalized.

The child psychologist was making the point that the boy knew intuitively what was wrong, and though he couldn't speak, he managed to convey the presence of the tapeworm in pictorial form. This remarkable story indicates the power of the protective body self to use imagery, whether in language or visually, to communicate its distress and its needs.

New Light   THE POWER OF WORDS

It might be helpful to watch for the descriptive words and images you use about yourself. Explore whether you do in fact think this way, or whether it is just a habit, asking yourself 'why?'. You can even ask your closest friends to tell you when you inadvertently put yourself down. As I have said, many remarks against ourselves go unnoticed, and we may not be aware of how self-punishing our underlying thoughts can be.

If you do find a pattern of words, images or thoughts which are judgmental, punitive or critical of yourself, you can explore where these might have come from, asking questions such as: 'When did I first hear this about myself?' 'What am I really saying about myself?' 'Is there a fear or hurt which causes this behaviour or characteristic I criticize in myself?'

Is there then a way in which you could let these negative statements go, releasing the hurt, and maybe even replacing these words with positive ones? Can you choose to be Jemma, rather than Joanna?

CHAPTER SEVEN

RECOGNIZING CHOICE

To let go or to change the way you think requires, as a first step, the courage to have faith in the self.

I ENDED the last chapter with a question about choosing what to think, but I fully realize that to believe that you have a choice, particularly when your emotions or patterns are involved, is very hard if you are not used to the idea. So can we really get to the stage where no matter what is happening, we choose what we think—choose to think positively about ourselves, for example? Or will the emotions and the patterns continue to run us?

Sometimes the mind seems to be preparing for the worst. For example, when we are fearful about something that may happen in the future, part of the anxiety is often that we do not believe we will be able to cope. People have said to me in the counselling situation: 'If that happens I know I won't be able to cope!' The mind creates visions of the worst possible scenario because, as I've said, that is its job: to make us explore all options by preparing us for the worst.

However, I have met people who have not only coped with extreme difficulty, but who in the process have found a greatness within themselves which has been *more than they could ever have conceived*. From this and my own experience, it is not the things that happen to us which seem, in the end, to matter the most, so much as our response to them—our inward response more than anything else. It is what we think about the event, or the situation, which matters and this in turn affects how we feel about it.

As you will read in chapter nine, in the section 'Another Light' (p. 170), I have had the privilege to be involved in healing work for many years. One of the first patients I treated had a painful gastric disorder. After a few treatments she told me that nothing had changed. The pain was still there—the physical condition remained the same. 'But', she said, 'I feel completely differently about it. The fear has gone'. This in turn affected the physical healing process. That was one lesson to me about how the power of our thoughts can affect even painful physical states.

In the heat of a frightening moment it may feel as if we have no choice whatsoever over how we think. We may feel the same when a condition has been going on for a long time, and seems to be out of our control. Sometimes the feelings of hurt or embitterment are so strong that the defensive self is uppermost; again, sometimes we feel so extremely afraid of what will happen, often of what we might lose, that the mind's defences take over. When emotions like fear and hurt-based anger are paramount, it is often extremely hard to choose to think differently. However, although we may have no control over circumstances, we always do have a choice as to how we are going to *respond*, if we can recognize what is happening. Our choice may apply inwardly rather than outwardly, on a moment-by-moment basis, and possibly only fleetingly, but it is there. The ability to choose is what the next few chapters address.

Dealing with 'Hypnosis'

HAVE you ever had a 'knee-jerk' reaction to someone or some situation? You say something, and afterwards you realize that you had no thought at the time, or maybe you are frozen and say nothing. It was almost as if you were in an hypnotic state. Events just seemed to unfold; words were said, then later you may have felt regret, even guilt. You maybe also felt frustrated, because you think now that you could have said it better.

To apply the word 'hypnotic' may seem overly dramatic, but at knee-jerk times it feels as if your true self is in abeyance, that something else takes over, and that you have no control over what comes out of your mouth or what you do. That almost mesmerized state of being is indicative of a strong defensive reaction. It is your protection asserting itself, and squashing all thought in the process. It is a mother springing to the defence of her child, no matter what the truth is, and no matter the dangers or consequences!

This kind of reaction does not only happen in a striking way. Indeed, it is more often a reaction in ordinary conversation, and some people who are very vulnerable live in such a state for the majority of the time.

As a way of explaining what I mean by this, we have elements of all possible over-reactions within us. We can all be depressed, for example, and for some that leads to chronic depression and even suicide. We can all be controlling, and for some that leads to dominating others regularly. So too with our fears, which for some can lead to a kind of paralysis, but for many of us just to occasional knee-jerk reactions. So, too, for lack of self-worth and anxiety, which for some people are so entrenched that they daily experience within themselves a lack of control or a confusion of mind. These then inhibit clear thinking.

When people describe to me times when they find themselves struck dumb or shocked or speaking without thinking, I ask them what they would like to have happened. Usually the reply is that they would like to have been able to think straight—even to think at all! They describe wishing they could have had the space to compose

---

New Light SPACE TO THINK

If you are tired of reacting, rather than responding to situations, if you long to have a choice, if you long to think differently, then give yourself that space to think *now*. When you do, the question to ask yourself is not, 'What do I want to say?', or 'What do I want to do?', but 'What is it I really want?'. Asking this question reminds you that you are not just the impulsive self that is hurt or afraid, but an intelligent person who has another, broader agenda, and who can also recognize that the situation is not what it seems on the surface, and nor is the other person.

In asking, 'What do I really want?', you give your person self the opportunity to choose, in a place beyond the knee-jerk reaction, beyond defensiveness, beyond fear. It may be that in the act of allowing space to listen to yourself, you find an answer to that question which is entirely the opposite of what you thought you might choose!

a thought-through response. What we then do is to explore the fears or hurts which maybe lie underneath the
reaction. Through doing this I am trying to give them a
handle on what is going on, to remove the guilt by seeing
the process, and to get to a point where finding space to
think is a possibility.

Obviously there are always going to be times when the
defensive self takes over, without thought, and if protection is required, then this is healthy. But in most situations
finding the *space to think* becomes a powerful way of regaining control and, most importantly, realizing that you
have at the very least a choice of what to think.

Courage

I SHOULD like to return again to one of the first statements I made in this book, about the body self's role in
life being to keep us safe. The perennial, often unwanted,
negative thoughts are, as I've said, only a response to a
perceived threat. It may also appear to the mind that to
let go of the mental anxiety or the anger is to give in—to
wave the white flag and feel the despair of loss of face
before our perceived enemies, or hopelessness before
the difficult condition of life we face. Yet the choice to
think differently requires great courage, and is not a sign
of weakness. We look at people like Nelson Mandela in
prison, and Laurens van der Post in a Japanese prisoner
of war camp* and are amazed and uplifted by their abil-

---

*See his books, A BAR OF SHADOW (1954) and THE NIGHT OF THE NEW MOON
(1970) which were the basis for the film 'Merry Christmas, Mr Lawrence'
(1983).

ity to think outside the norms of hatred and despair. We recognize this courage because we have it in us to do it ourselves. It may be that most of us will not have to face such extremes of pain and intolerance, but when you are trapped in the prison of your negative thoughts, to you it seems just as difficult to escape.

What does it require, then? **To let go or to change the way you think requires, as a first step, the courage to have faith in the self.** Your choice is to let go the misconceptions of the self as weak, ill, stupid, unlovable, wrong, and see rather the defensive self as a tool: one which can be laid aside and another chosen.

This in itself is a powerful action that can transform your mental arena, because in so doing you regain control. Rather than being led by what is a noble, but limited, body-self reaction, you the person take control of what you are thinking; you the person make changes. It is as if you suddenly realize that the key to the prison cell is hanging there all the time, and you have the power and the choice to use it to open the door!

Trusting the Way

I HAVE mentioned the importance of being able to access the past in order to release any locked-in hurt, and it is worth talking again about the importance of this moment. Yes, there is a time when we need to look back, but how do we know when that is? How do we know when to make a decision for our future?

Choosing at all requires courage and a level of faith, even if it's only an item of clothing we're choosing, or where to go for a holiday. There is always a measure of uncertainty, and perhaps we can all recognize the hesitation, the slight anxiety accompanying a choice. Of course, we cannot control the randomness of life: the future may hold *anything* for us. We cannot plan for every eventuality that lies ahead. It would take an extraordinary chess master to consider all the moves through to the end of the game from the first one. Some people become paralyzed by uncertainty, others react and regret later. The fear of the body self stops us flowing and creates rigidity, in an effort to control our environment and to feel safe. So how do we deal with the uncertainty of life?

How many times have you got into a stew, or a rush, only to find that everything then conspires to frustrate you further? In contrast, when you've gone with the 'tide' of events, you may have been aware of what seem to be miracles of timing, coincidences and events all supporting your flow.

Anything rigid that is placed in a flowing river, whether it be a material object or a thought, sets up a backwash—a turbulence around it—which affects the flow and creates frustration and side-eddies, in which energy is trapped and buffeted about for a while. It might then be harder to see the way ahead: a set idea or a strong desire, even an aim that does not allow flexibility, is like a rigid mass placed in the stream of one's life and consciousness. Rigidity arises out of the defensive self. A barricade is made rigid and firm to withstand the onslaught of the tide. However, nature also shows us that a tree has to be flexible in order to withstand the variable strengths of the wind. And this is the point: change is variable and unpredictable. We cannot know the outcomes of events, or predict the responses of others, so being flexible in our approach to life is crucial.

Writers often describe the state of mind when inspiration comes to them as open and almost like a daydream: a fluid state of consciousness in which they are 'in the flow'. Jazz musicians talk about getting into a rhythm where their bodies and movements seem to be part of the world around them and playing seems easy. Healers and counsellors use the language of becoming one with their clients' or their patients' energy, and artists of being one with the subject of their painting. All are slipping into a stream of awareness where they are not resisting the tide but cooperating with it, and where all things are flowing together in the rightness of the moment. I am not just referring to heightened states of awareness, but to everyday consciousness, and how this impedes or facilitates our actions, movements and the outcome of our endeavours.

Maybe you have found, as I have, that pushing, manipulating, resisting or agonizing all set up a vibration bringing frustration, hold-ups and problems. By contrast, relaxing into the moment sets up a different vibration, where events seem to flow with you, and you with them, as if everything is supporting you. In what seems to be an odd way, the vibration of relaxation seems to mould the energy field around you, causing life to appear different.

Living in the moment is a way to remain open to whatever occurs and to respond accordingly. Far from being apathetically resigned—'*I suppose I'll have to put up with it; I must accept my fate!*'—this way of being is challenging, fun and powerful. It opens us up to the possibilities that each

New Light LIVING IN THE MOMENT

To practise living in the moment, it may seem an obvious thing to focus first on what is around you and within you right now. Spend a few moments simply looking at what is there, and just feeling what you feel. Often in rushing from one thing to the next we are not actually living with what is, but with what is coming, and what has been. Practise being the athletes mentioned earlier—completely focused on now, no matter how repetitive or unexciting that might seem to be. Notice the colours of things, the perfumes and sounds, and the sensations that arise within you.

Close your eyes after a while and watch what arises in your mind without judgment. Feel the release of tension in yourself as you allow everything to be, without the need to compare, judge, condemn, struggle to control, resist or explain it all. Just watch and listen.

After a while you will find the spaces between inner events, thoughts or feelings will lengthen, so that you will be watching and listening in more silence and with a greater feeling of stillness. However, don't anticipate this, just keep on being inwardly aware.

This practice of what is sometimes called 'mindfulness' can lead not only to a place of peace, but to a way of living which is more conscious and ultimately more effective.

(You many also like to use the creative visualization in Appendix I, called 'Riding the Waves of Change' (p. 174), to develop your power to trust the self in each moment.)

moment presents us with.

But what is the power of the moment? I have mentioned words like 'vibration', but what does that mean? To me there is a way in which when you trust the moment to teach you, when you trust the flow of circumstances and of life, what you are really doing is trusting *yourself* in each moment. Our modern cultures are haunted by spectres of failure, so that we think we need to push, manipulate and struggle in order to get anywhere, or even to stay in the same position. They do not help us at all to trust ourselves in the moment.

There is a difference between agonizing over the past and exploring the past. There is a difference between planning for the future with flexibility, and fearing the future. The difference is in emotional relaxation and the trust of the self, which I shall call 'the inner thread'.

Keeping Hold of the Inner Thread

ONE OF the reactions of the defensive mind is to imagine that a situation will last forever unless we keep going over and over it to try to find a way out. However, that going over and over is like a ball of string we are trying to unravel externally by pulling at it this way and that. It becomes more tangled the more you tug in frustration!

To trust the inner thread does not mean a situation has to last forever. To let go, into the flow of life, does not mean giving in. When we resist, it is often because we feel out of control—powerless to doing anything about a situation, unsafe. We need to trust that if and when we can change something, the opportunity will present itself. Always our choice and our power lie not in what we can do, but in how we respond inwardly to what happens.

We might compare the present moment to a labyrinth.

We do not know what is around any particular corner, what each new step will bring. In mythology, when seekers entered the labyrinth they took a thread which they unravelled as they went, as a guide for their return. Going with the flow of the moment is a powerful way to live, and the thread that is your safety is *your own self-belief*. The inner thread is what you hold onto, and keep running all the time.

Another image would be a stabilizer on a ship. One wave yields to another, but the inner stabilizer, your faith in your self, means you are not buffeted, but remain calm, poised, unshakable inwardly, while outwardly riding the waves. This is what allows you to respond to some situations creatively and to others constructively. It is not a surrender to inevitability, but a conscious, confident grip of each moment as it arises; an openness to the small inner

---

New Light POSITIVE AFFIRMATIONS

If you find yourself feeling frustrated or agitated and you know you are resisting the flow, you may find it helpful to repeat to yourself some words that will remind you of the power of non-resistance. Some people find this approach helpful, especially if they like using words, or often have negative thoughts running in their head. Substituting something positive can enable you to reconnect with your person self and release the pattern. In this case affirmative statements like the ones below can be useful.

'I trust myself in this moment'

'I work creatively with what is open to me in this moment'

'In my integrity I am strong'

'I resist nothing; I hold on to nothing'.

promptings which come in that moment, a use of all the senses really to 'see' what is happening and judge what is an appropriate response. If there is something to be done about a situation it will present itself to us inevitably, and at exactly the right moment. If we are aware and prepared to flow, then we will automatically deal with it, and our dealings will seem to flow.

Staying Still

AFTER talking about going with the flow, I am fully aware that sometimes there is a choice or a movement we know we could take, but do not. For example, when we are hurt by someone we may find we have enough space eventually to realize we can let that hurt go, but we do not want to do so. I am sure everyone remembers situations where part of you knows you want to let go of a destructive way of thinking, for example, yet instead you cling to your feelings.

This resistance to change, to moving on, even towards acknowledging there is a choice, is something I'd like to present in a positive light, especially since I have noticed that a lot of guilt gathers within us when we know we are resisting. I should like to take the idea of the protective nature we all have and look deeper at what is happening. Part of the defensiveness of the body self can be a refusal to move or see possibilities, but the reason for this is that *we do not feel safe enough at that moment.* The anxiety is there precisely because the pillars of self-worth within are not yet strong enough for us to take down the scaffolding.

To return to the situation where we feel someone has

hurt us, in such a case it is natural to cling to our feelings until the body self feels its self-esteem is no longer under threat. Resistance is merely a sign, then, of lack of safety.

What I have experienced is that when someone who is resisting is allowed to do so, without any feeling of being in the wrong, *that very demonstration of respect will gradually melt the defensive posture.* They will—*of their own accord*—seek to move forwards again. I do not even like to use the word 'resistance' in my mind, since to me it is only a way of maintaining self-respect in the face of a perceived threat. The body self is doing its job, and will stop 'resisting' once the threat is withdrawn.

Not only do we need respect, sometimes we require active encouragement from others to know that we are OK. Statements like: 'It must be really hard for you right now', can help. So too can acknowledgment of how difficult it is to choose the 'person', rather than the 'pattern' when we are still in pain.

Power Released

TO KNOW you have a choice either to stay still or to go with the flow requires that you feel empowered. However, many of the ways in which people feel threatened are around issues of feeling disempowered. To feel you are not worth anything, to be *afraid*, to lack confidence, or to be consumed with guilt, are all states of being which are disempowering. A person's power comes from a strong sense of self—not a defensive sense of self—an inner knowing that he or she is good, or to use an alliterative phrase I like: **loving, lovable and lovely**!

New Light GIVING THE AFFIRMING RESPONSE

When someone feels hurt by you, if there is the possibility to re-act to their hurt with an acknowledgment of their feelings, with-out patronizing them, then it will go a long way towards releasing pain, allowing genuine communication about the real issues, and coming back to a place of goodwill. It is difficult to say something like: 'I'm so sorry I've hurt you', but I have found it can open up all kinds of psychological 'doors' if, at that moment, you can let go of the need to defend, and see the need of the other per-son for understanding, beneath their accusation. To say you are sorry about their hurt is genuine, even when you feel justified. Your person self will not wish them pain, and by reconnecting with this part of your being, you show that you are both seeking to do your best.

What you are seeking is for you both to be able to move forwards from a combative stance to one of reconciliation. The most important thing under such circumstances is the tone of your voice. It is not so much what you say, but the tone in which you express it which will be healing. A voice which is full of genu-ine remorse for another's feelings will help. This is because what the person most wants at such a time is for their pain to be heard and acknowledged. 'I am hurting' is what they are saying, and a response that is sympathetic in tone will allow them to move into something larger than the hurt.

If you are the one in pain and find it hard to let it go, try thinking that not choosing to move on arises simply because you are not feeling good enough about yourself. What will help you is not self-chastisement but seeking and finding the support for your self-esteem that you need.

Can you say that you feel loving, lovable and lovely? Many people I have talked to, and in a variety of situations, especially when they are feeling hurt enough to seek a counsellor, do not feel loving, lovable or lovely at all. Indeed, in my experience many of the problems that they and others are beset with arise from this. A preponderance of guilt means one does not feel a loving person, or very lovable. Relationship or work problems or issues around self-confidence may prevent you feeling lovable or lovely. Being afraid or anxious produces defensive behaviours—ones that we do not like very much at all.

The inability to separate out protective behaviour from the person self means that people often see themselves as ugly, unlovable and not very nice. You only have to add cultural attitudes towards age, looks and body weight to this, and you can slide into a deep well of disrespect.

Any negative views of the self sap the will. Those who are trying to lose weight or give up smoking, for example, are not only working against their desire to eat or smoke, but against the strong feeling that they are not worth it, lazy and ugly. This is why so many self-help books will focus on accepting where you are now before you can move on. However, it is not just a question of accepting, which can slip into resignation, but of changing the whole perception of what makes one *loving, lovable or lovely*.

Immense power comes from knowing you are precisely that—loving, lovable and lovely—no matter what you look like, and no matter how you think or feel. That is a hard thing to get our heads around! All the things we do not like about ourselves are the things which are part of our protection—lovely in their own way, even—but there is also a self which is being protected, and that self is **strong, tender, kind and beautiful**.

It is worth mentioning here that it is a sad reflection on our society that any man reading this may still find words like tender, beautiful and lovely hard to relate to! A man who has looked after a baby, though, will inwardly understand those words more easily, even if he would prefer not to use them in relation to himself in conversation. It may also be the case for men, as much as for women, that they can understand the feeling of power that comes from tenderness in intimate relations, or again when looking after a young child. At such moments, the other person is fully dependent on you, and fully loving of you, and with that comes a strength and a will to good which can make you feel invincible! No wonder being in love is so intoxicating!

New Light IN LOVE

Can you imagine or remember a situation where you were in love? Can you take yourself into that inner world and feel what it is like, or could be like? Doesn't it make you feel powerful? You feel you can do anything and put up with anything. Nothing is beyond you because your image of yourself through your lover's eyes is of someone who is loving, lovable and lovely!

Immense power is released through love, and this is as true of love of the self as it is of love of another. The reverse is also true of course. So can you empower yourself now, even though you may not at this moment be in love with another. Can you feel for yourself the kind of respect and positive regard a lover would? In so doing the insecurity of the body self will go and then all the power of your being will be released to you.

Supporting the Will

ONE OF the reasons for my bringing up the issue of em-
powerment is that without any sense of one's own power
it is harder to have the will, or the continuing will, to do
what you want to do, whether that is to effect change
within, to focus on something clearly or to stay in the
present. With regard to making changes, for example, it
is easier, in some ways, to keep things as they are. The
impetus to change and to effect changes has to be strong
and enduring, and one often needs some kind of support
to see it through.

The will is the use of the inner energy of the being—
emotional, mental and physical. When we will to do something, then time, energy and space all are geared behind
the event. Sometimes the use of the will is unconscious,
as when we are doing something out of love, but when
we are conscious of it there is a sense of focus, maybe of
present-centredness, or of one-pointedness, of energy or
strength, of determination and the ability to endure.

Many things can sap the will:
>   tiredness,
>   chronic illness or pain,
>   depression,
>   fear or anxiety,
> negative thoughts of weakness in any form,
>   lack of self-esteem,
>   guilt,
> impatience resulting in our overextending ourselves,
>   and consequent failures (not knowing our
>   weaknesses and our strengths).

Lack of support, possibly active criticism and resistance by others all sap the will, too. Inner statements may be made by the person like 'What's the point anyway?', or 'I can't', or an attempt to make things better through saying, 'Things are not too bad, really'.

One of the strongest ways in which the will is compromised is fear of change, with all its projected consequences. You may have experienced how long it takes sometimes to make a life-change, especially if there is no obvious right way, or if other people may be hurt in the process. As I've said, in counselling this can cause a variety of protective behaviours all of which one might be tempted to call 'resistance'. Sometimes the person hides the fear because they feel guilty about it, especially when the change is something they want. Sometimes a person may be angry with their counsellor or not turn up for their session.

It is important, whether you are a counsellor, a person in counselling, or just facing a crucial change or choice in your life, to address the fears that may be there, without shame. It means understanding that any voluntary change takes a great deal of courage and persistence, and that there is every likelihood that for some time a person may not be able to go forward, but that each time there is seeming failure it is an opportunity to check whether the change proposed is really wanted. **There is nothing wrong with changing one's mind!**

If I may speak for a moment of the counsellor's role, to me it is vital not to have any vested interest in outcomes, nor to believe we know best. If you do, then when the person does not do what you feel is right you are going to feel personally let down, or frustrated, and then you are not going to be there for them. This quality of supporting the person, no matter what, has, to my mind, much more of the attitude of serving, rather than helping. It does not matter whether the person does this, or that, or nothing, only that they are feeling supported in their struggle. So, again, the more one addresses the self-worth of a person and helps them to believe in themselves, the more they will have the will to effect the changes that are right for them.

Tiredness and lack of peace can also be an important area for people to look at when it comes to lack of will. Lack of peace can cause all of us to feel irritated and impatient, and can mean that we lack resistance to fear, that we lose the ability to endure. It also dissipates energy, and the focus we need for the will to be fully utilized. For some people, the ability to relax is as important a need as getting enough peace or sleep.

Anger is an emotion that may initially stimulate your desire for change, but if you are stuck in that anger, then

---

New Light SELF-ENQUIRY

Useful questions you may ask yourself about supporting the will to change include:

    What will support me in this?

    What are my fears about this?

    What would make me give up?

    What thoughts/words will help me to keep going?

    When the will is threatened or absent, there is some fear or hurt that is getting in the way. Find what that is and you will go a long way towards releasing all the energy you need and finding the right focus.

it can have the reverse effect by sapping the will. Arguing, fighting, complaining and condemning take the place of doing something about it. It is good to know the difference between will and anger. Will is a fusion of the decisive mind and the needs, whereas anger is an emotional reaction to hurt, which I looked at more fully in 'Dealing with our Anger', on p. 61.

It is important to allow the anger full expression, without judgment, if it is there—but it is also important to understand what the hurt is that underlies the anger. In other words, it is primarily the hurt that needs to be heard, and when it is heard the defensive self—from which the anger comes—will be able to let go and allow the strength of the individual to take over. It is my experience that many people find themselves exhausted by their own anger, and I believe it is because the hurt is still there to be heard, and until that time the will to change is blocked by it. It is in some ways like a baby who will not stop crying until it is fed, or had its nappy changed! It knows exactly what to do. It is a healthy reaction, though it may be painful to hear, and it will stop when its needs are heard and met.

Rediscovering Self-Belief

AS THIS is the last topic of a chapter which is entitled 'Recognizing Choice', I'd like to summarize the ground we've covered. I have mentioned many times the need to trust the self and the importance of self-belief. I hope that through what has been said, the reader will have discovered how a change in perception of the self can help to reinstate this confidence. If so we can move on to the final part of the book, which tells how we make this work in relationship to others.

First, I'd like to make clear that although I have mentioned a distinction between the patterns—the defensiveness, the things we do not like in ourselves—and the person, in no way do I see them as separate. It could seem that I am postulating a dualistic notion of the self, but in fact **it is important to see the self not as split, but as integrated.** The body self—the mind, body and feelings (senses)—are there to keep us safe. This is an automatic, primal reaction, which is necessary and useful. Sometimes reactions to a threat on the part of this automatic self can become fixed, responding to events in the past that are no longer happening, and the reactions are no longer appropriate—these are the defensive patterns. However, at all times the innocent, pre-threat person is present, though sometimes veiled.

The reactions to threat can be so strong as to occlude the whole of the self. The understanding to draw is not that there is a part of your being working against you, but that sometimes a person does not realize how powerful, intelligent and in control they truly are—a thought that takes us right back to the beginning of the book. You can unveil that greater self through gaining a different perspective on the things you do not like in yourself.

Secondly, part of that new perspective comes from understanding the nature of learning and how failure is part of growth. This includes a different picture of what is happening when things appear to go wrong. Through this awareness you begin to be able to live with the defensiveness, without guilt, while at the same time you may seek to change it. Trying to live without guilt or fear of failure is a further way to increase your self-belief.

Thirdly, further new understanding is gained when you begin to see yourself as a unique individual, without comparing yourself with others. This is a powerful change of perception, because it can remove the barriers you have assumed are inhibiting your creativity, intelligence and ability. What you think has value, because no one else has your perspective. *What you create* has value likewise. There is no need to judge your ability against another's. You can have confidence in your opinions because they are as valid as anyone's, without the need to try to change others, or fit it with them.

Finally, part of that change may come about through finding those initial painful events, which are often restimulated in the present, and releasing the locked-in feelings which are still operating your defence mechanisms. As the defences release, you reconnect with your inner joy, strength, intelligence, peace and love. It does not happen all at once, but because you understand failure now, when mistakes happen you see them as part of a process. You see them as a sign of hurt or fear, and they do not so easily knock your faith in your self. You seek to release the hurt or fear rather than become despondent and lose confidence.

A baby has complete self-belief, in that there is no sense in it of failure or guilt. It responds to the moment and to its own needs, and its innocence gives us great pleasure. Perhaps we recognize, in that baby or very young child, something which we know to be true of personhood, but which often becomes veiled—that we are all innocent, worthy beings?

CHAPTER EIGHT

MAKING THINGS WORK

To know yourself as incomparable is to increase your ability to relate appropriately with others and to make things work.

EARLIER I asked the question, 'What do you really want?'. A further question might be, 'Do you want to make things work?'. When you want to make things work, you broaden your outlook to include all aspects and all people in a situation. You move away from the defended self towards uniting all in the project, the relationship, the job, the family, the community, the country, the world. I was once staying in a community where the residents needed to put up a very large telegraph pole. At first it was impossible to lift, but the group began to focus together and sing together, until through their togetherness they managed to raise the pole. The same process can go on within our self.

In this section I want to write about making things work. It is perhaps axiomatic that many of the times we find ourselves becoming defensive are in relationship to others, and it is certainly in relationships of all kinds that the focus of 'Making Things Work' will be important. At work, in the home and among our friends we find the greatest challenges to our emotional stability, as well as the greatest opportunities to be self-fulfilled.

It may be worth looking back at what we have shared about the uniqueness of each individual, since the change in viewpoint given here is very much about accepting the premise that to know yourself as incomparable is to increase your ability to relate appropriately with others and to make things work. What this awareness of uniqueness does, in relation to others, is to help you have confidence in your own perspective so that you can listen to others and share with them.

In arguments between people, one of the basic problems is that both sides appear to believe, sincerely, that they are right. It is my experience that when you look deeper, you realize that our inability to hear, and still less let in, the other person's point of view is based not on a firm belief in our own rightness, but the threat to our integrity which seems to be implied—and vice versa.

You may have experienced this. You may have found that you have held on to your side of an argument long after you can see the other's point of view—not because you are contrary, but because it would seem to diminish you if you show you have changed your mind. I perceive it as depressing that when a politician changes his or her mind about something, which is not always an unreasonable thing to do, the media react with ridicule. Far from being cause for derision, it seems to me that on these occasions the person often feels strong enough, confident enough in their own values, to be able to appreciate the viewpoints of others, and that is laudable. It is indeed *what makes things work*.

What is True?

AS I'VE said, part of the problem with difficulties in relationships centres around who has the truth. You may have heard statements like, **'This is the way it should be done'**, **'No, you never helped me when I asked you to!'**, *'How can you say such a thing, when you know it wasn't like that!'* or *You must be right because I'm always getting things wrong'*. There are others, such as 'I don't want to make a mistake; what do you think I should do?', *'Of course, I'm so dim, we'll do it your way'*. In all these instances the person involved is on the defensive, either in being determined to be right, or determined he or she is always wrong. Because they are defensive, people will argue and fight for what they believe—or else give in to others and fail to find their own voice, which may then allow resentment to run strongly underneath.

It may be obvious to say that an increase in confidence will help the person who feels they are always wrong. However, for those whose defence is the determination to be right, you might think that an increase in confidence would make them even more dogmatic and more convinced of their own rightness. However, if you look back at the times when you have felt confident, you might find that what happens is the opposite.

If there has been any time in your life when you have felt quietly confident in yourself, you may have discovered that because of this confidence you have felt able to be more tolerant of others and their opinions. This might have been a moment when you were in love, for example, and you could tolerate the parts of your partner you did not agree with simply because you felt loving towards him or her, as well as loved. That in turn brought a feeling of safety, so that you could be flexible and open without feeling you were losing face or position. You did not feel threatened. In other words, your defensive self was in abeyance, because love made you strong in your person.

It is when we feel insecure in ourselves and lack faith in our unique truth that the defences arise. When we feel insecure, we need to make others agree with us, because that is a way that we can be sure we are right. It is the insecurity in us that makes us feel the need to judge others, or to make them believe the truth that we see. If we truly believed in what was right for us we would not need to make others do the same; we would be able to say, in effect: **'I respect what is right for you; I don't need to prove you wrong in order to be right myself, and here is what I think'.**

In the same way as each is unique, each of us has our own truth: truth that is right for us, and comes out of our own history and our own needs for learning and growth. This does not mean that we cannot learn from each other, or find places of common ground within our differences. Imagine standing in the same room with many people, all with their own angle on truth, and feeling relaxed about this. Then you may be more able to look around and say, `Well, maybe I could use that` or `I wonder if that is true for me, too` or `Now is it possible I could expand my understanding a bit with what so and so believes?`. Thus we are open to others, and open to learning from them if it feels right for us. At the same time, we do not feel we have to agree with them in order to make everyone happy.

Truth is Fluid

MOSTLY, we know that in order to make things work with others we need enough fluidity to be able to share and to listen. When we lack confidence we tend to become rigid and uncompromising. This of course means that in disagreements it is harder to find a place where people can come together to make things work.

Confidence, in short, enables us to see that truth is not fixed. Sometimes what limits us is that we hold on too tightly to a past bit of truth, and in our insecurity we are unable to let go. We do not open up to what is happening and what we are seeing now, and that may in fact be showing us another layer of truth. With self-confidence, each moment is an opportunity to grow and to see things differently. With self-confidence, you do not feel diminished because you change your mind, find another way to look at something, or accept that in fact the other person has a good point.

In relationship counselling the pain is sometimes so great for each partner that the defences are enormous, or so I have found. Then it is hard for either of them to see over to the tender flowers beyond their partner's walls. When one person, out of their own hurt, argues vehemently for their truth, the other feels equally backed into a defensive corner, where they feel so threatened that their own wall of truth grows higher. Fortunately, it also happens that if in some way one person finds what I call a 'back door' open to them—that is, they are enabled to find a way of releasing their insistence without losing face—then the other person feels able to let their own defences down a little. The skilled counsellor finds all kinds of creative ways to enable this process—whereby each person begins to feel safe, without loss of face or self-esteem. If you are trying to make things work with someone, then it might be helpful to bear this psychological process in mind, so that seeking ways to create safety for the other person will be a means to your goal of making things work.

One to One

THE WHOLE of this section is made up of ways of working that you can put into practice when you want to make things work between you and another person. I shall refer, though, both to one-to-one situations, and also to the therapeutic or counselling situation, as I believe each could inform the other.

The starting point is that you want to make things work. Whatever the relationship between you, you want this meeting to work appropriately. During the course of your encounter, and particularly when things get sticky, if you can take your mind back to that premise it will help you avoid slipping into defensive mode. Or it will help you get out of it, or make a back door for the other person to slip out of theirs.

The idea that you want to make things work also takes some of the heat out of the situation. It might be worthwhile spending a short time beforehand asking yourself the question, 'Do I want to make things work?'. By this I mean, do you want the discussion or encounter to work, not necessarily that you are hoping for a particular out-

come or longterm change. Having focused on making it
work as your aim, it is easier to remind yourself of your
intent when difficulties arise in the dialogue.

Another thing to bear in mind at this stage is that you
cannot change the other person, or outwardly influence
anything they think. But by keeping yourself as free of
defensiveness as you can, and focused on making it work,
you will have an influence on the situation as a whole.
This is because you will be creating more safety and, as
we have seen, when someone feels safe their defences relax. It is subsequently easier to talk without emotion stopping the words from coming out the way you would like,
and to hear the other person without feeling threatened.

It is worth thinking about this dynamic a bit more.
The problems in communication often arise in those two
ways. Lack of safety means a negative emotional response
and that produces defensiveness. The emotions of protectiveness and hurt can sometimes be overwhelmingly sudden, and at other times they can hardly be acknowledged
outwardly. On those occasions we cannot find the words
we want, or simply lash out in a way which we subsequently regret—because it was not really the point of the
argument. In other words, our lashing out expressed how
we felt, but not what the underlying problem was. Next,
the argument revolves around the hurt feelings on both
sides, and the tangle produced means that the real issues
do not get expressed or looked at. Afterwards we feel frustrated—or, worse, that we have betrayed ourselves. At the
same time, if there was lack of safety, it will have prevent-
ed us from hearing what the other person is saying. We
cannot then recognize that what they are saying is their

opinion—even that it is their truth—but that we have our own, which is just as valid.

This is where we need to return to the nature of truth and confidence in our own integrity. I believe that when we have the safe space to see that there is no ultimate truth, but that ours is just as valid as another's and both can be right, it helps us to relax and hear that truth for what it is.

Listen

ONE OF the ways in which you can really help the other person feel safe is to demonstrate that you are listening to them. This seems obvious, but the kind of listening I am referring to is where you create an honest environment of 'Tell me how it is for you'; not one of, 'I'll tell you how it is for you', or 'This is how it should be for you'. In other words it is **a way of listening that is without any agenda except that of hearing what is being said**.

If your relationship with the other person is primarily an emotional one, this will be harder to achieve, but if you are able to remember that simply listening in this way does not diminish you or make you 'wrong', you may be surprised at how much the other person will respond positively. When anyone really feels they are being listened to, they are able to relax their defences and not only speak from their true feelings, but are able to hear themselves as they speak. Obviously, when you listen to another person in this way you do not rush them forwards, or interrupt them with your thoughts or questions however valid. You give them space as well as emotional security, and it allows them to monitor inwardly what they say, to make internal adjustments and reach conclusions.

To prevent both of you slipping into argument, you can also set up the time together agreeing a certain length of time for each to speak, while the other listens. In a counselling situation this is invaluable. It helps each party to value the time they have, for the counsellor does not want the person simply to regurgitate what they think their counsellor wants to hear, but to gain self-realization.

Respect

THE KIND of listening I've described has, as its basis, respect for the other person, in spite of your differences. The harder the issues between you, the harder it will be to hold on to respectful listening. Your own hurt or self-protective feelings will get in the way of your respect for the other as a person. You may have had the experience of mixed thoughts and feelings when in an argument with someone—a love/hate mixture. But this example can show you that underneath the hurt there is still respect, no matter what has happened, and it is that which you are seeking to keep to the fore, despite your hurt. One way to do this is again to remind yourself, once again, 'I want to make this work'. Another is to acknowledge that though the hurt is there, the respect can be there alongside it. Keeping in your mind the notion that the person is only acting from their own defences, and that behind that barrier is as tender a person as yourself is one way of allowing you to remain open to them.

In counselling, when a person is lacking in respect for themselves, this respect shown from outside has a profound effect on them. I have noticed that when someone is vulnerable, anxious, in confusion or pain, they generally lack respect for themselves too. Part of the counsellor's role, which again is an RC notion, is to model respect for the person until they can rediscover it for themselves. You believe in them, and they will begin to accept that they are still worthy of respect. Yet it was a Freudian psycho-analyst, Peter Lomas, who said: 'To be open to someone means that we are receptive to her being, that we let her disclose herself. One feature of this state of mind is humility. We do not assume that we know, that the other has nothing to teach us, that she will not change us. Our attitude will be one of respect or reverence. Such words … are necessary if we are to convey the kind of receptivity likely to do justice to the complexity of human beings.'*

Two Intelligences

ONE WAY in which this respect is achieved is by the counsellor having the thought in their mind that there are indeed 'two intelligences working together'. Although this may never be voiced, there is a way in which (to quote Lomas again),† 'The best help we give others is through our quality of consciousness, rather than a vast armamentarium of techniques'. How we are thinking about someone comes across to them in a variety of ways, without the need for words—tone of voice, manner, eye contact and facial expression being a few. But there is also a more subtle permeation, which influences the whole discourse, from the outwardly obvious to what you choose to see and hear, and what you chose to say or the way in which you phrase a question.

*THE LIMITS OF INTERPRETATION, p. 39. †same page

What we have to remember is that those who come to us for counselling help are very likely feeling at their most vulnerable, and therefore their sensitivity to any kind of negativity will be heightened, and particularly to the way in which they are perceived by the counsellor.

Ongoing development is something all professionals engage in, and in the Appendix I have given some supportive material that counsellors may find helpful. The questionnaire there may also be useful for anyone who wants to explore their feelings and thoughts.*

Safety Creates Honesty

IN ANY one-to-one situation, particularly where there are challenges and emotions running high, people need to feel safe to unburden themselves and really to be able to say what they feel and think. In such situations, as I expect you have noticed, people can be nervous of exposing themselves both mentally and emotionally, and therefore feeling even more vulnerable. Feeling safe is consequently necessary for healing to take place.

Where things are difficult in a one-to-one situation and you wish them to work, here are some guidelines. You wish for resolution and to be able to come back to a place of goodwill between you, so creating safety for the other person (as far as you are able) means that they will be able to look at the emotions and thoughts which underpin their reactions and not feel the need to

*Ideas for looking at your relationship with the person are set out in Appendix II, 'Two Intelligences or One?', where the questionnaire 'For Self-Exploration' is designed to help uncover a variety of attitudes and feelings.

hide behind any kind of bravado, or veils created for self-preservation. With understanding of the need for safety in order to allow the defences to relax, coupled with the knowledge that when they do the person, not the body self, will 'appear', you will find that the situation loses any sense in which there is a battle going on, or one person is dominating or forcing revelations on another.

I believe, and have seen, that to do all in your power to set the person at their ease, knowing that this is the best way forward, brings the best results. The person may even seem to be lying, prevaricating. They may be aggressive, they may avoid and resist, but once they know they are respected as an equal partner in the process, that will change. Indeed, it is my experience that resistance needs to be met with a stepping back, so that the other person can step forwards. John Heider in his excellent paraphrasing of words on leadership from the *Tao Te Ching* of Laozi, puts it thus: 'Gentle interventions, if they are clear, overcome rigid resistances. If gentleness fails, try yielding or stepping back altogether. When the leader yields, resistances relax.'* Though Heider's is a book about leading groups, I have found that many of the sayings in it are applicable in any relationship situation.

In an interpersonal relationship it is so easy to attribute attitudes and motives to the other person that prevent you feeling their equal. It is a common reaction to feel dominated or powerless. What will help things work is if you can recognize that the other person feels as powerless as you, no matter how they are behaving. Indeed, the more defensive they are, the less powerful they will be feeling.

*THE TAO OF LEADERSSHIP, John Heider, p. 85.

It may well be much harder to step back if emotions intervene, and yet the understanding that if you can create more safety for your partner, they will be able to engage more creatively with you, can be a help. It may also help to remember that your partner's so-called 'negative' reactions are not the whole of them, or even the truth of how they are feeling, but only a response to feeling unsafe.

Taking your Cues from the Other Person

REALLY listening for what the other person is saying will always help to make things work. That is perhaps self-evident. If there are difficulties between you, then you will have an agenda (things you want to say, feelings you want to express) and it is important not to lose sight of the agenda items—but if you are determined to make things work it is crucial that rather than each person simply offloading, you try to work together to sort out the problem.

What happens is that we panic and think that we will not have the opportunity to express all we want. However, it is my experience that if you listen to your partner, ask questions or share things based on what they say, and let them lead the conversation, pretty soon they will begin to feel relaxed enough to let you share more. One person has to break the deadlock of tit-for-tat defensiveness, in order to create the safe conditions for dialogue.

In order to do this, if you take all your cues for what questions you ask from what the other person says, so that they really feel you are listening to them and not simply waiting to jump in with your own issues, then it is not only respectful and trusting but also, in my experience, the most skilful thing to do. When someone feels heard, they allow themselves to hear themselves. When that happens, opportunities for self-awareness blossom and they begin to trust you, and are more prepared to hear then what you have to say. You mirror how you wish to be listened to in turn.

If you need to ask questions about what has been said, try to keep your tone of voice neutral rather than accusatory or defensive. If your tone of voice has no expectation of a particular kind of response, then it will not arouse the defensiveness of the other. If what you say, or your manner, seems in any way to be attacking, minimizing, patronizing, or judgmental, the person may well start to defend their position in order to make you understand— to make you hear and respect them and their feelings. As soon as you feel the need to defend a position, then a continuing position to defend is created, and the harder it is to leave it.

Sometimes it may seem as if the other person is extremely controlling or is actually in control. This is their safety net, if so. Attack it and you will be compounding the feeling they have that they need to be in control. The walls will grow, like those flood barriers I described early in the book. When you see someone being aggressive, you know that underneath they feel insecure. When they give the impression of being very controlling, that is their means of survival.

Someone once said of their extremely controlling husband that he would be lost without his controls. The wife had wisely seen the underlying insecurity that produced the strong need to be in command of everything and everyone.

One of the strongest incidences I have had of trusting the person, not the defence—in this case in a therapeutic situation—also involved the power of imagery. This individual revealed to herself, through her drawings of violence, the trauma of childhood abuse that she had completely occluded—that is to say, hidden. As we worked together, she began to share these drawings with me, as well as dreams and feelings, until one day she began to remember what had happened to her. She later had this confirmed by a member of her family. Total self-protection, complete occlusion of the kind she had devised for herself, is sometimes necessary to preserve sanity. To do this may help the child self in some ways to feel secure, but when the time is right and the conditions of safety are in place, the adult will allow themselves to release the pain. The urge towards health is always there.

New Light PRACTICE MAKES PERFECT

One way of practising these skills, in preparation for the problem times, is to do so when the heat is off! In other words, in your ordinary conversations with people, try practising the ideas given in this section: the ways of listening, asking questions, taking your cues from them, making yourself a safe person to be with, and so on. You may find that all your encounters become

---

Understanding Outbursts

LISTENING, respecting, believing in equality, finding common ground and creating safety are all aspects of skilful communication, and I believe are achievable in order to make things work. Much of what I've written in chapter six, 'Liberating the Voice', may also be useful. However, keeping communication going in the face of hurt is not always easy, and it is therefore worth going back to something touched on earlier (when we discussed mindsets, p. 83), which is the explosion of unconsidered words—the sudden defensive reaction which can arise in any communication.

When you witness an explosion, it can be helpful to see that there was a build-up of feelings which have suddenly found an outlet, and that they are not all to do with you. When it is you that explodes, the words you regret do not come from you the person, neither is the outburst from some totally inaccessible part of you, but rather a sign that you are feeling threatened in some way, and the circumstances of the moment have triggered the feelings—actually, allowed them to come out. Something in the present has re-stimulated feelings from the past.

I believe this way of seeing what is happening is helpful in a number of ways. To begin with, it allows the opportunity, whether you are the speaker or the one who listens and hears, to look at what has been said with less likelihood of blame. Something has been set off which is not necessarily to do with the present moment, or the people involved.

Here's an example. Jo has exploded with wrathful words. Josh is stunned. However, Josh has triggered a patterned reaction in his partner, which is more to do with an historical event in Jo's life than to do with him. Indeed, Jo has allowed herself to let go in this way because actually she feels safe with Josh.

When I use the word 'allowed', you might ask why, if the words have suddenly come out without her willing it, can Jo have 'allowed' them to? Whether you call it cultural control, or whether you think, like me, that it is the basic goodness—an ethical immanence—of the person, we nonetheless actually do control the outpouring of our defensiveness, and release it only when it feels safe to do so. The point is not to see this as a personal threat. If we could see some of the 'communication' that comes our way as an offloading of a more general unease, it could help us not to react in return, or feel criticized. Some partners handle this really well, as most of us have occasion to see, from time to time.

So there is a way in which this release of emotion, in the words Jo uses, is a good thing. It alerts her to the fact that something is in need of attention—some part of her is hurting, and it allows out some of the hurt which may well have been gathering momentum within.

In sum, far from being frightened or hurt by the sudden outbursts of our friends, or our own self, there is a way in which we may be able to see these in a positive light. Of course, the outburst may not be the end of it. Jo may want to take a deeper look at why she said what she did. What were her fears? From where did they come? When did she first feel like that? Josh may want to celebrate that he did not react to Jo even though he felt stunned, but was there for her, and he may wish to find ways to help her feel more safe. If he does this, Josh may find that the floodgates open and Jo releases a lot of emotion, but ultimately this will be very healthy. Nonetheless, he needs to be prepared to receive without fear.

New Light PREPARING FOR THE OUTBURST

The next time someone shouts at you, or is coldly hostile, take a few deeper breaths and try to remember that their outburst or hostility may not all be to do with you. You may offer the line of least resistance for them, an opportunity to offload a build-up of pressure. In some ways you may be the safest person they know.

This realization may not make you feel that much better right then, but it may help you not to feel pushed into guilt.

It is also helpful to practise this kind of scenario in your mind and how you would like to respond.

Other People's Tears

IN COMMUNICATION around difficult issues, we often have to deal with another person's tears. We do not always feel comfortable about this, and I believe the discomfort can be eased by changing our perception of what is happening when people cry. Since hurt and fear lie at the heart of our defensiveness, crying is one of the ways in which we release them. Crying is sometimes—to use a gross but effective analogy—like taking the head off a boil and allowing what is there to ooze out, until the wound is cleansed. Crying is a release of tension, and also an expression of relief.

Even with that understanding, though, many people still have a problem with other people crying. It can cause all kinds of protective responses in oneself, unless you really do accept its purpose and its health-restoring properties.

Some of those difficult reactions to tears may arise because tears in others stimulate our own urge to cry, yet we have discomfort around doing so. This means that instead of being there for the person crying, we can become rigid and tend to move away, or try to stop the tears as soon as possible. So many times I have heard people—either on stage or screen, or in life, say things like: *'Don't cry. It will all be alright'*. What would be more helpful would be to say: *'Don't worry about crying. I am content for you to do what you need to do right now'*.

Other protective reactions to someone crying can arise from the fear that the person will not stop. Yet it is my experience that people are much more likely to stop themselves crying than to go on for ever! They will cry until the wound—for that present moment—is clear. Their crying will not go on forever, precisely because it is a means of release. A negative reaction on the part of the listener can also be because they think that crying is making things worse, when in fact it is a sign of healing, not of entrenchment of emotion. **Crying is not the pain, but the release of pain.**

When someone you know is crying because of a bereavement, a frequent thought is that you do not know what to do to help them. That feeling of helplessness also prevents you being there for the person. When someone is bereaved, there is obviously nothing you can do to bring their loved one back, and so you get the sense that there is nothing you can do at all! This is partly because action is the body self's regular way of making something better. When no action will work, we have a tendency to feel we are not doing anything.

What a grieving person needs most at that time is for the tears of loss to flow, and for someone to be there for them, holding them and allowing them to express all their pain. To do this, and continue to do this for the bereaved, will be offering more than you may believe. The same is true with someone who is themself dying. Elisabeth Kübler-Ross's work is still, to my mind, some of the best for those who wish to help people who are facing death, and in ON DEATH AND DYING she says: 'Dying persons will welcome someone who is willing to talk with them about their dying, but will allow them to keep their defences as long as they need them.' In this statement she suggests three of the most important considerations I believe people deserve, which are:

- to be able to express their pain,
- to keep whatever protection they need for as long as they feel they need it, and
- to be treated with respect.

Someone who is allowed to cry will more quickly come to a state of equilibrium. However, the tears for a present hurt often become a vehicle for past hurts to be released as well. To give a simple example, if you are crying for the loss of your mother, and you were not allowed to grieve enough for your father who died earlier, you may find that you are crying to release the loss of them both. It does sometimes seem to the onlooker that there is something unnaturally dramatic happening, which can in turn make you feel nervous. When you witness someone crying more than you feel is necessary, or in a dramatic or sensational way, it is helpful to remember that they are likely to be releasing the past.

Another reason for dramatic crying, a quantity of tears that seem inappropriate to the present loss, can be that the person is asking that their pain be heard. Sometimes, the hurts and fears of childhood are not heard enough. Children will inwardly tend to blame themselves for all kinds of things that are not their fault—for family break-ups, for example. Children can suffer terrible bullying they never report, or they may report verbal bullying that is not seen as important by adults. Children can feel deprived of love, or have too many expectations placed upon them, so that they feel useless when they fail. The hurts and fears can build up over the years, the pain unheard and unreleased.

The body self is always looking for a means to release pain, though, so that any trigger of those feelings can produce tears. Without the ability to connect those tears with past events, the person may not realize what is happening. There needs to be help to understand where the hurt is coming from, so that changes of perception can occur that will allow the person to feel whole in the present. In this case, part of what you do when you allow the person to cry is that you let the 'child self' know that it is heard.

People also relate to me how they have cried on seeing something beautiful, or something which reminds them of love. To me that is a sign of recognition of their person, and the personhood of each member of the human race; also a sign of the goodness and loveliness of life, where it has perhaps not been seen for a while. Suddenly, you are reminded that life is something more than defensiveness and all the difficult feelings and reactions that can bring. What these kinds of tears can also be is a vehicle for the tears of hurt to also be released—but again, this is a means to restore health.

Allowing tears to be released whenever they arise can deeply release tension which a person may not realize they are carrying inside. Sometimes the physical illnesses, mental depressions and oversensitivity we experience can be as a result of this locked-in anguish; these unacknowledged fears, which can all be brought to the surface and healed.*

New Light THE GIFT OF TEARS

It is a great gift we give someone when we allow them to cry. It is a gift we can also give ourselves. Are there things you wish to cry about?

If you immediately think of something when you read these words then perhaps now is the time to let it happen.

To do this, ask a good friend—someone you know respects you—to simply hold you and let you cry, without saying anything to try to make it better, but with confidence, warmth and respect for you. If they are really good at this, they do not even need to know what it is you are crying about.

The Cultivation of Imagination as a Tool

YOU MAY be surprised by the inclusion of this topic, but the cultivation of the imagination has an important benefit in one-to-one communication, in that through its use we begin to be able to look over the walls that hide others from us. We begin to be able to put ourselves in each other's shoes, and to imagine what might be going on inside for each other, instead of just reacting to surface behaviour and appearance.

Cultivation of the imagination is vital. If we simply react to what is on the surface, we are living on the surface of life, using only our earthly senses and never developing

*For an idea of some steps to follow when you feel someone has hurt you, see Appendix I.

deeper awareness. Then we never see beyond the cultural norms of thinking or the prevailing pop psychology. In relationship terms, if we always react to the surface of life, we are often perpetuating fear and hurt, because we are not understanding what the other person is trying to tell us. We are not comprehending how life really is for them. So we need to learn how to respond to something *beyond* what we see and hear.

I want to be clear that this does not mean putting words into other people's mouths, or telling someone what they are thinking or feeling, which is disrespectful and patronizing. The use of the imagination is more for our internal understanding: to help us be open to the fact that someone may be operating on the basis of fear, which then causes the barricade to go up. You build a coastal dyke because you fear the devastation the sea might bring, not for any other reason. To be aware that someone may be afraid, and to imagine what that might feel like to them, helps us set that person at their ease and diffuse situations of misunderstanding or conflict that could escalate. As well as imagination, this takes the ability to remember (to imagine with hindsight) what it was like for us at similar times in our own lives, or to imagine ahead how we might feel.

When someone is reacting negatively towards us, we can see before us a defensive barrier built of fear and hurt, rather than who that person really is. We may not always be able to see that someone as a wonderful being, but we can cultivate the awareness that what is on the outside, if defensive, is often the opposite of what is happening within. The barricades are up, and the person is not revealing themselves. That much we know easily, once we have begun to think.

We can imagine, if we wish, that over the dyke is a field full of beautiful, tender flowers, which we would never wish to harm. We may then find ourselves doing whatever it takes to allow that person to feel less threatened, and thus perhaps reveal who they truly are. We may find ourselves stepping back metaphorically, and releasing our own automatic, defensive response; we may begin to understand the other person's concerns; we may say we are sorry; we may offer to talk; we may be still and listen; we may begin to find resolutions and compromises which affirm both us and them.

Gradually, of course, our task is to learn to take down the defences we build as vulnerable children, or as adults who have been hurt. Gradually we learn that if the waves the sea rushes in the waves don't overwhelm us: we can swim, and nothing can destroy us or truly harm us. But that takes time. Meanwhile we have to live with our own defences, and other people's flood barriers, but we can imagine and believe in what lies behind them, both for other people and for ourselves.

New Light FACING THE CHALLENGE

Take into your imagination the most challenging people you know…. Can you imagine that what they seem to be on the outside is the exact opposite of what they feel inside? See the garden the other side of the flood dyke. Take a few moments to imagine first how they might be feeling to cause such behaviour as you encounter outwardly, and secondly, how they might be if they felt safe and loved.

CHAPTER NINE

HOW WOULD YOU LIKE TO CONTINUE?

My hope is that this book has given you a new and positive light in which to view yourself, but whether you agree with that viewpoint or not, here is one person who believes in you, no matter who you are!

I T GOES without saying, almost, that despite the similarities in events that happen to us and the thoughts and feelings we have, we are each one in a different place on our own path of growth. What is right for one, will not be so for another, and so the responses to the ideas and exercises in this book will be varied. I can only offer what has worked for me, both personally and professionally; in the end, what matters is that you find what works for you.

If the ideas in this book resonate with you and you wish to continue to use them, you may find helpful the summation of the contents of this book that forms the next topic. How you use this list will be as individual as you are, and it is in no particular order. If you are at a point where you like to be systematic, you might choose to work on each one of these in turn for a period of time, revisiting the corresponding sections in the book, and any exercises therein. If you like words, you might make up a positive affirmation for one or more of the statements on the list, which you repeat regularly in order to change your viewpoint of yourself and to move forwards. You may like to use the list to revisit the past, and release the hurt you might find there in tears. With all however, I think it will be helpful to remember what has been written about the nature of expectations and how we learn. If you are going to use this list it is also helpful to reread the section: 'Make Sure you feel Safe' (p. 49).

My hope is that this book has given you a new and positive light in which to view yourself, but whether you agree with that viewpoint or not, here is one person who believes in you, no matter who you are!

A Checklist of Useful Skills and Practices

- Creating safety for self and others; remembering vulnerability.
- Not expecting too much.
- Speaking to the person; seeing through their pattern.
- Saying how you feel, not blaming.
- Responding to the moment, not the history.
- Remembering your uniqueness.
- Not comparing yourself with others.
- Letting others be.
- Avoiding generalizations.

- Deciding what you think; remembering the nature of truth.
- Letting go limitations.
- Contradicting any punitive, critical, destructive statements you say about yourself.
- Releasing past hurts and fears and allowing them to release in others.
- Cultivating strength within so that walls lower naturally.
- Supporting the person, understanding the patterns of defence.
- Asking, 'How can I make things work?'.
- Believing in the goodness of people.
- Cultivating living with uncertainty, living with mistakes, living with a process of learning.
- Forgiving the self, letting go guilt, coming back to innocence.
- Remembering that what on the outside is often different from what is inside.
- Giving people back doors to get out of or stepping back to help them lower their defences.
- Respecting yourself.
- Looking deeper than the surface reactions, and being aware of triggers.
- Believing in yourself; cultivating self-esteem.
- Allowing tears and understanding anger.
- Believing in your intelligence and creativity.
- Empowering self and others.
- Freeing self and others.

Remember 'that we are powerful beyond measure… And when we let our own light shine, we unconsciously give other people permission to do the same. As we are liberated from our own fear, our presence automatically liberates others."

A Checklist of Strategies for when You have felt Hurt by Someone

• RELEASE the feelings of hurt in some way—talk, shout, punch cushions, cry.

• Re-empower yourself. Write a letter to the person which you do not necessarily send; practise speaking out to them how hurt you are and how you are worthy of respect; make a list of all your qualities worthy of respect; list why this person should have respected your humanity, or your feelings, your role, your skills and expertise, or your person. Remember that this will work best if you keep in mind the fact that you are not blaming or punishing, but reclaiming your own power.

• From this position of reclaiming your own power, you can reclaim your own self-respect and then your will.

• From a position of self-respect you can then return to a position where goodwill can be re-established between you—where you can reclaim respect for them as a person. With self-respect you do not collude with their defensive behaviour or submit to it, but you regain your centre and your understanding, from which you can ask yourself, 'How can I make things work from here?'

• At this point you may contemplate how the defensiveness or the habitual reaction may have arisen. This does not have to be the true story as it is for the person—you may never know that—but it is a reminder that all kinds of feelings may have been happening for them internally which are nothing to do with you or this moment.

• If this is not the first time this has happened, remember how hard it can be to get out of one groove into another, and that the *person* will be trying to do so. They may never show you that they are trying—their fears of losing face or guilt may well get in the way.

• Remember the image of the flood dyke and the flower-filled pasture behind it. Until the person feels safe the defensive pattern will keep on arising. There may be things you can do to help them feel more safe—to find ways to do this will increase your awareness of your own integrity.

• At another time, without any self-judgment, seek beneath the surface of your hurt reaction to find what fear or insecurity in you has been triggered. Simply acknowledging that fear will be helpful, and then you can find ways to release it or minimize its power to affect you in the future.

Facilitating a Group

AT SOME point, you may find yourself volunteering or even paid to run a group, whether it be to look at some important issue people have an investment in, or to allow growth in the participants. In this section I should like to offer some help to those involved in group work. Although this section is geared towards the facilitator, groups are by nature participatory, and I think that anyone involved in a group will find the ideas helpful.

I have facilitated many and various groups over the years, from groups of teachers discussing their feelings about being in the classroom, through yoga classes where feelings are shared to retreat groups with specific themes. I have been at trustee meetings, with groups of people in a variety of skills and in a training situation, and in groups formed to carry out projects. Gradually I have developed a way of working with a group that I believe embodies the philosophy and psychology expressed in this book.

Here are the tips I would offer.

•   Try to be clear about the aims of the group and state them at the beginning. Different groups require different kinds of work and participation. However, consider what the purpose of the group is, as well as its aims. What I mean by this is that the functioning of the group is as important as its outcome. Indeed the quality of the outcome will depend on how much each person within the group feels heard and valued. It is not up to the facilitator to 'set people right'. Respect the fluid nature of truth within relationships, and that each person has their own truth.

•   Consider what it is you want the participants to be feeling. Is it safe, secure, loved, relaxed, respected and therefore open to what the group brings and what each might say? The safer, more relaxed, and less challenged people feel, the more they will feel able to share or ask questions. Therefore set up the conditions in the group such that everyone feels safe. To begin with, this can be done simply by stating it as your intention.

•   It is as well to remember that going round an untried group asking for people to share could create distress, and instead it may be best to offer the opportunity to share without putting anyone on the spot. In a group some people take time to feel ready to share, or need plenty of time to absorb rather than speak. Two further skills are therefore involved: that you trust the participants, seeing yourselves as 'several intelligences working together' and yet each one unique, and that you can find appropriately non-threatening ways of interrupting someone who is repeatedly holding the floor for too long.

• Be clear with the group from the outset about the boundaries you want to create, and the things you wish to avoid happening. For example, you might say: 'If I interrupt you when you are speaking, it will not be because of what you are saying, but simply that I am aware of the time and the number of people in the group'.

• Another way to set the boundaries for safety is to ask people to speak as if they were putting something into a large pot in the middle of the group, from which the listeners can take it if they wish or not—using 'I', rather than 'you'. This avoids one member of the group telling another what they should be doing.

• Recognize that people are often more vulnerable than one believes from the outside. People can be shy and not used to speaking or even being in a group. A group situation sets up a challenge for people on many levels, not least of which is that you can usually all see each other. How many times have you experienced the situation in a public meeting where the front seats or the inner circle does not get filled?

• Recognize that people have a tendency to be defensive when they, or their beliefs, feel challenged.

Consider that if people need to defend they will not be open to the meeting, the aims of the group, you, or anyone else. Therefore, try not to stir things up, or become defensive yourself. This is difficult, but try not to be challenging or defensive even when your personal feelings are aroused. Consider that defensiveness escalates when people feel pushed into corners. Allow 'back doors', i.e., escape routes: 'Gentleness overcomes rigid resistances' (see p. 148). If people can 'keep face', they will more likely be able to hear, and be back in touch with their 'person'. Try not to embarrass or challenge any member of the group.

• Be clear about your attitude to the group. For example, 'I truly believe each one of us is unique and has a unique path to follow, even when we experience similar things. If we really think this way, there is no need for us to fight or argue with each other, but we can share from our own experience.'

• Be clear about your attitude to your role. Do you really consider yourself a facilitator, or that you are in some superior position? The role will vary according to the group's purpose and the rules of the meeting, but there is a way in which the more the leader can step back, others can step forwards, no matter what the aims of the group are. Showing oneself to be part of the group rather than separate from it enables each one to feel recognized. This is an attitude of mind, and a chosen attitude towards the other participants. It may be demonstrated in your demeanour and tone of voice, rather than how much you say. However, you also need to remember one of the primary aims, which is safety. If the facilitator does not grip situations which can cause others distress, does not lead when they need to, is not clear about process, does not have the skills to bring the group back to the main task at the *appropriate* moment, then there is the danger that safety will be compromised. The facilitator does not have to step back so far that they disappear altogether! The safety of the whole group is the leader's responsibility.

• Listen with real attention to each participant, but feel you can still steer the balance in the group, through the boundaries all agreed to begin with. Consider how much easier it is to feel heard by someone who is relaxed and open, and model this for others when you can.

• Keep a balance of attention in the group, considering that there is a group feeling that the facilitator needs to be aware of. This is something more subtle, but is a thing you may recognize if you have facilitated groups before. A facilitator gets a sense of the mood of the group as a whole, as well as individuals within the group. If that mood becomes too heavy then the work, whatever it is, cannot be done. Humour and comments about ordinary things can be used to lighten the atmosphere, so long as you are making sure this is not making light of anyone's pain or fears, of course. Here is another moment to remember that releasing tears is not the same as despair or hopelessness; it may itself lighten the group.

• Leading a group requires flexibility in thought and response, if one is truly going to believe in the uniqueness of everyone there, and trust them and the flow of the moment. If you resonate with this kind of approach then the book mentioned earlier by John Heider, THE TAO OF LEADERSHIP, is a useful one to read, and much within it can be applied to all kinds of interpersonal relationships, not just working with groups.

•   Consider celebrating the participants in a group whenever it is possible, without being patronizing or disingenuous. The difference will be felt in how much the person feels the remark comes from one learning soul to another, and not from 'on high', or from the 'leader' to the 'pupil'. I have also found that the more the use of positive affirmation becomes part of the leader's skill, the more real it becomes. I refer you again to the sections in this book about good teaching, and the misconceptions that abound about praise in this context. The ability to celebrate another's skill, gifts, work, feelings or words is one which is not generally fostered in a competitive society, except when people are talking about those they consider to be at the top. Being someone who enjoys watching a variety of sports, I have often heard commentators speaking with surprise of a sportsman or woman who celebrates the other competitors, rather than denigrates them. I long for this to be unsurprising because it is the norm!

Lastly, you may like to look at the second of the 'questionnaires' in Appendix II.

Another Light

ONE OF the effects of taking a new look at yourself, and particularly if this leads to self-realization, is that you begin to review how you feel not only about yourself, but about life itself. Confronting fears of death, for example, can bring you to the point of asking whether you think it is the total end of you or just a change of state. Thinking of yourself as a unique, creative being can bring you to question whether you think this is haphazard, or the result of some kind of plan which is not at the moment visible to you. Exploring the power of living in the moment and the power of your thought can make you consider whether what you can locate through your physical senses is all there is, and whether there are laws operating beyond those of physics. Reconnecting with your innocent, intelligent self can make you wonder if there is a purpose to your life beyond the material needs.

The conclusions we come to are necessarily as unique as we are, and for this reason I have written this book without much reference to any other dimension or belief system. It has been important to me to demonstrate that viewing yourself in this new light is not dependent on a particular kind of belief, other than a belief in persons—certainly not on any kind of spiritual or religious belief. In this sense the book remains consistent with how I would counsel, taking my cues from the person, and not mentioning any spiritual dimension except where the person has brought the subject up, and then only referring to their own beliefs, not imposing my own. However, here at the end, I would like, in the interest of openness, to share some of the conclusions I have come to as a result of looking deeper.

Previously I have mentioned my involvement with Transcendental Meditation, with Hatha Yoga (Iyengar School) and with Theravadin Buddhism. I have also been an orthodox Christian and have practised ZaZen. All of these experiences have been important in developing mental control and emotional stability, as well as in bringing an understanding that there is a level of reality which is beyond the physical, and which can influence it through meditation and meditative practices. More recently, but for the last thirty years, I have been involved with a spiritual organization which has been in existence since 1936 and which has evolved to disseminate the teaching of a being who calls himself White Eagle, after one of his earthly incarnations as a Native American Indian chief. Throughout all this time I have practised counselling, either one-to-one, or through teaching counselling skills in groups.

One of the aspects of the White Eagle Lodge that drew me to it was its emphasis on healing—healing for individuals, for conditions of life and for the world itself, and each person's ability to be involved with this. I am sure you can see how this would appeal to someone who had been involved with healing in a personal therapeutic sense for many years. Not only that, in White Eagle's teaching I met the same principles of respect for persons which I first encountered in Re-Evaluation Co-Counselling, and which has developed into a conviction through all my experiences with those I have counselled. In fact it was a personal and very evidential experience of how the laying on of hands (as it is sometimes called) can work, that made me consciously look for a spiritual healing organization in which to develop this ability.

The reason for mentioning this now is not to persuade you to join an organization or to promote any spiritual belief. Rather it is a way of being honest about where my work with people has led me. The people I have counselled and the stories they have told me have led me deeper into an understanding that life is not just this material body and world, but something far more, and that people are much greater, nobler and individually significant than we may be led to believe. Our media, as we know, concentrate in the main on the difficulties, the traumas, the horrors of life, and with more and more media outlets developing, right through to Twitter and beyond, we see more and more of the problems and the heartache. We see more, in other words, of the patterns of the defensive self, and not so much of the beauty of the person.

My work with people shows me something else. It shows me the unveiled person, the person without walls, the person who is loving, lovable and lovely. It has also led me to believe that this is our natural state of being—a spiritual state if you like—that we are reclaiming bit by bit. This has also been my experience in meditation and through healing work, that people grow towards the light because we are beings of light, not just here for a brief span and then gone, but eternal. Ultimately I have come not only to believe, but to see that even within a physical body self we are much, much more—'powerful beyond belief'!

APPENDIX I:
SOME USEFUL EXERCISES

WITH THE kinds of practices that follow, we are trying gradually to change the way in which we experience life. In the section on mindsets (chapter five, p. 83), you will read more about how we perceive things and how greatly the mind and the thoughts can influence even solid matter. There has been much recent research into mind maps, which through scientific investigation give credence to the power of the imagination to influence and increase achievement.*

In using the imagination, you may find your mind wanders. If so, gently bring yourself back as soon as you are aware of this to the image you have created. If you have to do this many times it does not matter. Try not to be anxious about this propensity of the mind because in so doing you set up a further barrier. The more you accept whatever is, the more you will be able to change it.

This may seem obvious now while you are reading this, but in your imagination you are always completely safe and the usual laws of physics do not apply. You cannot be hurt. Imagined scenes can seem very real, but part of its joy is that it is not like in a dream and you are in control at all times.

---

*See, for instance, Sandra and Matthew Blakeslee, THE BODY HAS A MIND OF ITS OWN.

Riding the Waves of Change

It is best to begin this imaginative exercise lying down on your back. A firm, but comfortable surface will normally allow you to relax without falling asleep. If you do fall asleep, consider that it is what you need to do. If you need to sit in a chair, that is fine. Take a few deeper breaths and release the tension in your body as much as you are able with each outbreath.

When you feel ready, picture a landscape in which there is a waterfall falling into a pool, from which a stream runs out towards the sea. Imagine that you can stand under this waterfall without danger. Feel the rush of the water as it pours over your skin. Let it drench you with both spray and sunlight; feel the continuous and eternal flow of the water. Remembering that you cannot be hurt. Allow the power of the fall to push you over and carry you down the river; go with the incessant surge of the river, and allow yourself to be tumbled along; let go of all your limbs and surrender to the flow—it is deep enough that you will not bruise yourself. At this moment say inwardly: 'I remain true to myself in the midst of change'.

The river empties out into the sea. Feel the movement of the waves under you, as you lie on your back. Experience the sensation of the waves moving under you, and your body riding them rather than being driven. Relax back on to the water. Feel the depth of the water beneath you, as gradually the tide carries you further out over the deeps. Say inwardly: 'I trust myself in the midst of change.'

Trust your strength and buoyancy on this sea of your existence. Do not be afraid of the depths beneath you, but know they are supporting you. Feel the waves beneath you: you float and flow, but you are never overwhelmed. You steer yourself through all the troughs and heights without resisting or clinging. Say to yourself: 'Through all things I am in control'. Feel the sensation of floating and being upheld by a strength and power that is not visible, yet there within you. Relax completely.

When you are ready to leave this inner world, imagine that the sea has gently left you on a sunny beach and receded. From this thought, feel the firmness of the floor or bed under you. Turn over and lie on one side. Rest. To come up to sitting, push yourself up with your hands from your side. Sit for a while before coming up to standing.

What you are seeking to do through this imaginative exercise is to reclaim your sense of integrity and strength, no matter what is happening around you. You are teaching your body self that you are safe. With that feeling of safety returns the feeling of power, opportunity, creativity and self-belief—which is your person self freed from fear.

Surrendering

BEFORE beginning this exercise, it is worth affirming that surrendering is not resignation, nor is it a response to hopelessness. Rather it is a process whereby you consciously move towards that which you most fear—in order, paradoxically, to remind yourself that you are in control.

Be somewhere where you feel comfortable, either sitting or lying down, and begin by focusing on your body. As in the breathing exercise given next, experience the sensation of letting tension go. There is a particular spot

half way up the neck between the skull and the shoulders. You can find it quite naturally if you think of a place
there becoming limp and loose, which will also enable
the shoulders and the brow to relax. There may be a feeling of release with your breathing, like a sigh, when this
happens. Imagine yourself surrounded by warmth, peace
and contentment.

Bring into your awareness the particular fear you wish
to deal with and visualize what it is connected with—a
person, a place, an event or an activity. See that subject
of your fear before you, yet some distance away. Now,
in your imagination, let yourself move towards that fear.
Move purposefully, even if you feel agitated. You may even
find yourself running towards it to embrace it. The mind
of the body self may find this disturbing or risible, but
keep moving nonetheless. Go right into the situation or
place, right up to the person or object and in full awareness let go of everything you can—all protection, all
thoughts about it, all defensive attitudes—almost as if you
stand naked before the object of your fear.

In that moment of complete surrender of the body
self, imagine another part of you becoming stronger, like
a backbone of light that cannot be shaken by anything
the fear now does. The more you surrender, the more you
find that place of still strength within.

What happens next is entirely in your hands. From this
rediscovered place of power you can choose to walk away,
embrace, speak, decide, listen or ignore. Whatever you do,
do it from a still place, an erect place, a controlled place
within yourself.

When you come back out of this visualization, try not

to analyze it too much, but instead to remember the sense of that inner poise in a way which you can call on again— a visual image, a word or a feeling—and which you can be return to whenever you remember and have need.

Conscious Breathing

This technique can be undertaken as a regular practice, but the beauty of it for me is that it can also be employed quickly in situations where one feels the need for calm. Although I discovered this for myself, after using the technique for some time I visited the website of a yoga teacher in New Zealand, Donna Farhi, who referred to a similar version of the practice, which she in turn had adapted from another teacher, Carola Spreads.*

It has been known for some time that deeper breathing techniques can have a powerful restorative and calming effect on many aspects of the body, however Donna Farhi in her book relates how the effects of 'straw breathing', which is what she calls this, are even greater.

For this exercise you can either be sitting or lying down on your back. You need to be comfortable, but the firmer the surface you can tolerate lying on the better. This actually allows the muscles of the back to relax more than a soft surface, and also allows the lungs the room to expand. When you lie down, do so with your arms a short way out from your sides and the palms upwards, and with something under your head so it does not tilt backwards. If you are sitting, it is helpful to be upright in

*See their respective books, Farhi's YOGA MIND, BODY AND SPIRIT and Spreads' WAYS TO BETTER BREATHING.

a chair, with cushions behind your back if you need support, rather than slouched, again so that the muscles can relax in as upright a position as possible without strain and the chest is free to move.

It is important to remember all that was said at the end of the section on 'Fear and all its Sidekicks' (p. 66) to do with feeling relaxed about focusing on your breathing. If at any time you begin to feel emotionally uncomfortable, then stop and take your mind off your breathing. This reaction may particularly apply to anyone who has had a problem with their breathing—for example, if you suffer from asthma. If in doubt at all about this, contact your healthcare practitioner for advice.

To begin the exercise, experience the sensation of the letting go of tension. If you have done the previous exercise, you will have found the spot half way up the neck between the skull and the shoulders from which your relaxation may spread. Think of that spot becoming limp and loose, and it will also enable the shoulders and the brow to relax. There may be a feeling of release with your breathing as well, like a sigh, when this happens. Imagine yourself surrounded by warmth, peace and contentment.

Just through your doing this, the breathing will naturally deepen without effort, and the whole point of this breathing routine is that it is without effort. The only attention you pay is to how you hold your lips. Adopt the position of the mouth that you would have if you were going to whistle. (This is the equivalent of holding a straw—hence Donna Farhi's name for this practice.) It need only be a gentle position, not too forced, so that you can hold it for as long as you want.

Breathe in normally through your nose and let your breath fall out through your pursed lips. That is all you do! The action of letting the breath fall out, yet through a narrower aperture than usual, has the effect of lengthening and slowing the exhalation. Because the exhalation is longer, you will naturally take a slightly deeper breath when you next breathe in. You can continue like this for as long as you wish, making sure that there is no forced inhaling or exhaling, just a natural inbreath and a consciously released outbreath.

If you wish you can add to this routine, once you are completely comfortable with it, and deepen your breathing more. To do so, take a normal inbreath, but when you exhale through your pursed lips, let the breath fall out for a little longer with each outbreath you make. Naturally your inbreath will be deeper too, but you do not need to make it so deliberately, just allow it to happen. Gradually you will get to the point where your lungs completely empty on the outbreath, and then the inbreath will be as deep as it can be.

At first, you may have a worry that you will not breathe in again if you let the breath out so far, but this will not happen. There may be a slight bump around the diaphragm area at the most empty point, and this will be the mechanism 'kicking in' to draw the air in again—it cannot fail to do so because it is an instinctive reaction of the body.

When you want to bring to an end any prolonged conscious breathing routine, all you need to do is to stop focusing on your breath. It will naturally be longer and deeper for a while after you stop. Just lie or sit still and relax until you feel ready to move. If you are lying down, roll onto your side to get up and push up to sitting from your side using your hands. Wait for a while, and then come up to standing.

Although this routine is one that can be done whenever you have the time, or regularly once a day, you can use the basic way of breathing in through the nose and breathing out through the pursued lips at any time you are feeling anxious or in need of calming. Simply take a few conscious breaths, in the way described, for as long as you feel you need, and allow the breathing to relax you, or bring you the space to be back in control.

APPENDIX II: QUESTIONNAIRES FOR SELF–EXPLORATION

THE FIRST questionnaire below is one I have used with groups of people who are developing counselling skills. The questions are designed to help the counsellor explore further their own person and their own patterns. The point is not that a counsellor becomes perfect, but that he or she has a growing awareness of the areas where they could become defensive within the counselling situation.

Whether you are a counsellor, or whether you simply like the idea of exploring your thoughts and feelings using this questionnaire, my suggestion is that you re-read the section 'Make Sure You Feel Safe' (chapter three, p. 49) so that you approach your answers with detachment, or so that you say to yourself things like: 'I wonder why I feel like that, and what fear/hurt is causing it?' The questions are a starting point for looking deeper and finding the positive, without guilt, blame or self-condemnation.

1.   In what situations, and with what kinds of people, do you find that you most often lack confidence?

2.   Do you feel empowered, or know what this means for you?

3.   Do you feel inferior to anyone, or in any particular kind of situation?

4.   How much do you feel an equal alongside your parents, or anyone you consider to be in authority?

5.   Do you have any persistent, negative thoughts about yourself?

6.   What criticisms of yourself by imaginary onlookers do you hear in your head?

7.   Can you accept the emotional side of yourself?

8.   What do you dislike about yourself?

9.   Do you feel most of the time you are being yourself, or true to yourself?

10. Are there times in your life when you 'shut off'?

11. Are there are grey, confused areas in your life, or in your self?

12. What kind of personality, fictional or real, do you most identify with, and why?

13. What kind of personality, fictional or real, do you admire, and why?

14. Is there anyone, past or present, whom you definitely dislike?

15. Do you periodically, or intensely, feel guilty about any particular event or person?

16. Can you step back when someone is saying something you disagree with, or do you want to argue?

17. When are you most gentle?

18. When are you most clear?

19. When are you most firm?

20. When do you feel most loving?

21. When do you feel most safe?

22. Do you feel safe and supported by life?

23. What frightens you, if anything?

24. What do you get most anxious about?

25. Are you frightened of death, dying, or growing old?

26. Do you feel out of control of yourself, or your life, at any time?

27. What thoughts do you seem to have least control of?

28. What areas of life, inner or outer, do you feel most effective in?

29. Is there anything in your life, past or present, about which you feel resentful?

30. List those things that you are currently working on in yourself.

31. What do you like about teaching/leading/being in authority in relationship to others?

32. What do you like about being taught?

33. If you have children, are you able to let go of them inwardly—to see them as souls in their own right, with their own path to follow?

34. If you have a partner, is he or she free in your eyes?

35. If you could choose to spend more time in the company of others whom you like, or more time in lovely natural surroundings, by yourself, which would it be?

36. Do you ever feel lonely, and/or do you like to be alone?

37. If you knew you only had one year to live what, if anything, would you change in your life?

Two Intelligences or One?

The second activity (it is not quite a questionnaire) is intended to help a counsellor look at the status of the relationship between him- or herself and the other person. (This means things like 'how do you feel about your relationship?'; 'who is or is not in control?'; 'what are your responsibilities?'; 'how much power you have and how should you exercise it?'. All these are questions the answers to which will dictate how you operate as a counsellor.

1. Think of someone who you believe to be in a position of authority relative to you, or someone from your past whom you thought of in this way. How did their authority come across to you, and how did it make you feel?

2. How do you react to people in positions of authority if they chastise you, or criticize you?

3. How do you react to people in positions of authority when they ask you to do things?

If you have never thought about this part of your inner world before you may not realize that you could adopt a style of relationship based on some of these patterns whenever you are in that role, or when things are difficult. Again, your defences may be re-stimulated, and simply to take a look at the possibility could be helpful.

APPENDIX III: BOOKS
MENTIONED OR RECOMMENDED

Blakeslee, Sandra and Matthew, THE BODY HAS A MIND OF ITS OWN. New York, NY (Random House), 2007.

Casement, Patrick, ON LEARNING FROM THE PATIENT. London and New York, NY (Tavistock) 1985.

Farber, Leslie, THE WAYS OF THE WILL. USA (Farber) 1966.

Farhi, Donna, YOGA MIND, BODY AND SPIRIT. New York, NY (Henry Holt) 2000.

Fromm, Eric and Suzuki, D. T., ZEN BUDDHISM AND PSYCHOANALYSIS. New York, NY (Harper) 1960.

Guggenbühl-Craig, Adolf, POWER IN THE HELPING PROFESSIONS. Dallas, TX (Spring) 1971.

Halmos, Paul, THE FAITH OF THE COUNSELLORS. London (Constable) 1965.

Harper, Ralph, THE EXISTENTIAL EXPERIENCE. Baltimore and London (Johns Hopkins) 1972

Harré, Rom, THE SINGULAR SELF. London (Sage) 1998.

Hayward, Anna, and White Eagle, LIVING WITH DEATH AND DYING. Liss, Hampshire (White Eagle Publishing Trust) 2002.

Heider, John, THE TAO OF LEADERSHIP. London (Wildwood House), 1986.

Jackins, Harvey, THE HUMAN SIDE OF HUMAN BEINGS. Seattle, WA (Rational Island), 1978.

Kennedy, Eugene and Charles, Sara, ON BECOMING A COUNSELLOR. Dublin (Gill and Macmillan), second edition, 1990.

Kübler-Ross, Elisabeth, ON DEATH AND DYING. London (Tavistock) 1970.

Lomas, Peter, THE LIMITS OF INTERPRETATION. Harmondsworth, Middlesex (Penguin), 1987.

Mearns, Dave and Thorne, Brian, PERSON-CENTRED COUNSELLING IN ACTION. London (Sage) 1988.

Moorhouse, Geoffrey, THE FEARFUL VOID. London (Hodder and

Stoughton) 1975.

Pert, Candace, MOLECULES OF EMOTION. London (Simon and Schuster) 1997.

Rodegast, Pat and Stanton, Judith, EMMANUEL'S BOOK II, THE CHOICE FOR LOVE. USA (Bantam) 1989.

Rogers, Carl, ON BECOMING A PERSON. London (Constable) 1961

Rowan, John, THE REALITY GAME. London (Routledge and Kegan Paul), 1983.

Sorrell, Stephanie, DEPRESSION AS A SPIRITUAL JOURNEY. Alresford, Hampshire (O Books) 2009.

Tillich, Paul, THE COURAGE TO BE. London & Glasgow (Collins) 1952.

van der Post, Laurens, A BAR OF SHADOW. London (Hogarth Press) 1954.

—, THE NIGHT OF THE NEW MOON. London (Hogarth Press) 1970.

van Deurzen-Smith, Emmy, EXISTENTIAL COUNSELLING IN PRACTICE. London (Sage) 1988.

White Eagle, WHITE EAGLE ON LIVING IN HARMONY. Liss, Hampshire (White Eagle Publishing Trust) 2005.

Wilber, Ken, Engler, Jack & Brown, Daniel, TRANSFORMATIONS OF CONSCIOUSNESS. Boston and London (New Science Library, Shambhala) 1986.

Williamson, Marianne, A RETURN TO LOVE: REFLECTIONS ON THE PRINCIPLES OF A COURSE IN MIRACLES. London and San Francisco (HarperAudio), 2004

Wilson, Timothy D., REDIRECT: THE SURPRISING NEW SCIENCE OF PSYCHOLOGICAL CHANGE. London (Allen Lane), 2011.

Wittgenstein, Ludwig, ON CERTAINTY. G.E.M. Anscombe and G.H. von Wright (eds.), G.E.M. Anscombe and D. Paul (trans.), Oxford (Blackwell), 1969.

INDEX OF 'NEW LIGHT' EXERCISES

INDEX OF PROPER NAMES

INDEX OF TOPICS